The 'Good Book' of FACTS & TRUTHS

GURU Number SEVEN

The 'Good Book' of Facts and Truths, GURU Number SEVEN

A unique book of fascinating facts and tantalizing truths bundled up in a double-barrel story.

A Guru-guided-tour of the world around us, appreciating the truth about facts and the facts about truths.

A story that kindles hope, and shows direction to all who want to catch the 'missed bus'; and get going.

Self-Published by author,

VINAY CHANDE

B.Arch. (MSU-Ind), M. A. Arch. (UF-USA), F.I.I.A., F.I.V.

Year 2021, Mumbai, India.

Title:
The 'Good Book' of FACTS & TRUTHS,
GURU Number SEVEN

Author:
Vinay Chande

Designed by
Vinay Chande

Publisher:
Vinay Chande
6-B, Horizon, Pali Hill, Bandra West,
Mumbai 400050, India.

Printer:
On-Demand Publishing LLC.

ISBN: 978-93-5445-067-9

Publisher's Note:
Effort has been made to ensure that the information contained in this book was factual at the time of going to press. Nonetheless, the publisher/s, the editor/s and author/s cannot accept responsibility for any errors or omissions however caused; as well as for loss or damage occasioned to any person acting, or refraining from action, as a result of the material in this publication.

CONTENTS

- *PROLOGUE.*

THE APPETIZER - a random collection of facts in a common format.

GURU Number SEVEN

- The Need and the Innovation.
- Initiation

TREASURY of FACTS & TRUTHS ... ...

- Interlude (Why include Truths?)

... cont. ... TREASURY of FACTS & TRUTHS.

- Clarification
- Reality
- Justification
- Lessons learned
- Compendium

- *EPILOGUE.*

A Fact is everybody's truth.

A Fiction is nobody's truth.

Myth is somebody's truth.

And it is a fact that

you can have your own truth.

⌑ Prologue

Nowadays, the success or the absence of it, divides people into 'Achievers' and 'Nonachievers'. I have observed that many nonachievers are actually intelligent, and are otherwise capable. Among these 'clever' non-achievers, there are you, the teenagers, the young adults and the unfortunate elders; who keep thinking "I have missed the bus, and I am never going to accomplish anything". I propose to address this 'thinking' through this book to kindle hope, and show direction to all who want 'to catch the bus'.

Statistics confirm that fascinating facts always amuse, entertain, educate, and bring a smile of self-assurance on everyone's face. A 'Book of Facts' has always been attractive to everyone, including your age group. Thus, I have maintained 'Facts and Truths' as the medium for this book.

Many have written books of facts; I also have. These books have a single purpose; to entertain and to get the reader GK smart. Maintaining this purpose, but as secondary; the main purpose of this book is to inspire, direct, and make aware. In this way it has become a dual-purpose book.

Hence, I have designed this book with a new concept, a unique identity, and multiple points for views.

The published books of facts, including mine, have made me aware of:

"When you know a little;
You know;
How little you know."

And this realization, tells that every typical 'Book of Facts,' has only a tiny slice of the infinite cake. It can never be 'complete' even by adding hundreds of more Facts. Thanks to the infinity of facts, none of the books have a beginning, an end, a wholeness or an identity.

And this book has to have wholeness and an identity, if it were to make a serious attempt to fulfil the main purpose of this book; i.e., to inspire, direct, and make aware.

In most creative processes, it is not possible to clearly state the process of solving problems; and it would be so here. As an architect, I am familiar and comfortable with this situation. You will have to wait till you use your solution.

My architectural experience confirms that if questions are stated in the right perspective and well understood, they brighten the light at the end of the tunnel. And that the process of correct orientation to a new problem, is certain to place one on the highway towards the solution.

You will see further down in the book that I have used the above-mentioned creative process lessons in the creation of this book.

Experts say that Improving awareness and alertness should be part of the goal of every 'good book' about self-help or success. I agree and have accordingly selected the special point of view.

With the point of view established, the perspective chose the angles and the script of this book started taking shape.

The following emerge as the directives:

"I must find a fresh way to place the facts and truths; almost in the form of a novel; which ties together places and characters in a unique way."

"My book should not just tell, but enlighten each reader with the rationale of the facts and the reality of the truths. And most importantly; kindle hope, and give direction to the reader for personal aspirations."

For choosing the format of this book; my teaching days at the colleges of architecture provided the clue. Then, I had observed that teachers who demonstrate; reach out more successfully. I intend to do the same here. I plan to place myself as a rudderless lost person seeking answers. And tell how I got on course to achieve my goal and be happy.

The emerging form of the book is unique. To digest the difference of this new form; an appetizer should surely warm things up. The appetizers here should get you into context, and give you a ready reference to compare (and enjoy) the typical existing format used by books of facts and that of this book.

The appetizer is a small collection of Fascinating Facts from my book in the conventional format, "The Book of Good Facts".

Vinay Chande

THE APPETIZER

A small random collection of facts in common format. These are all good facts. You will surely enjoy them. Please do.

I have placed here just enough numbers to give you a context and scale to compare with the main treasury and be aware of the relationship with the infinity of facts.

- When your mother was born, she already had **the egg, that would become you.**

- **The Eiffel Tower was originally intended for Barcelona, not Paris**. The Spanish city thought the design was ugly; so Mr. Eiffel took his idea to Paris, and succeeded.

- **The most ridiculous reason for being late:** The Russians showed up 12 days late for the 1908 Olympics in London, because they used the Julian calendar instead of the Gregorian.

- **Handshakes** were introduced to ensure that the person you were meeting wasn't carrying a concealed weapon. The had to be empty for a handclasp and the shaking was to dislodge weapons if any was hiding up the sleeve.

- In France, it is legal to **marry a dead** person.

- **Human male foetuses masturbate** from their days in the womb. Although female foetuses are also suspected to masturbate; aroused boys are the only ones who get caught via ultrasound.

- Every **'C'** in the name 'Pacific Ocean' **is pronounced differently.**

- **Which planet has the largest number of moons?** It is Saturn and not Jupiter. With recent discoveries of 20 more moons; the tally of moons for Saturn has gone up to 82; 3 more than Jupiter's 79.

- Box Jellyfish has 24 eyes; **the maximum number of eyes** in the animal world.

- **Starfish can regrow their arms**. Sometimes, a single arm can regenerate a whole body. Starfish has one eye on the top of each branch. They, however, cannot see color.

- Some **lions and dolphins** can mate over 30 times in a day.

- FORTY is the only **name of a number** which has all its letters in **alphabetical order** and ONE is the only number name with its letters in **reverse alphabetical order**.

- **'SMILE' was born in the 16th century.** The ability to smile is new; approximately five centuries old. Before the 16th Century, men and women, could not and did not Smile. **

- **Cleopatra was actually Greek, not Egyptian.** While Cleopatra was born in Egypt, her family origins from Greece. Her father was one of the generals of 'Alexander the Great'.

- **Male Horses** and rats **do not have nipples**. All other male mammals have nipples.

- Spanish **national anthem,** 'Marcha Real' **has no words**. It is one of the four national anthems in the world along with those of 1. Bosnia and Herzegovina, 2. Kosovo, and 3. San Marino that has no official lyrics.

- The abbreviation/label **'AD'** is placed before the year number; however, **'BC'** is placed after the year number (as: AD 2018, but, 68 BC).

** The validity of this finding is detailed in my published book - "THE SMILE, THE GAME CHANGER".

'Which language did the prophets speak?

Moses definitely spoke the 'Ancient Egyptian' (which became the Coptic) and the local vernacular language. Moses also spoke the '(old) Hebrew'.

Jesus primarily spoke the 'Aramaic' (the local vernacular language) and the 'Hebrew' (the spiritual language of the time). He spoke a limited 'Latin' and likely knew some 'Koine Greek'.

Mohammad mainly spoke the 'Arabic'. He also had rudimentary knowledge of the 'Greek', the 'Aramaic' and the 'Coptic'.

Buddha spoke the local languages; the 'Magadha Prakrit', and the 'Pali'. He also spoke the 'Sanskrit', the language of the aristocracy and as the language used in formal religious texts.

Confucius spoke a dialect of Chinese language which no longer survives today. It was very different from the present Chinese languages.

- **The Sun is** a yellow dwarf star. The temperature at its core is about 27 million Fahrenheit (15 million Celsius).

- The **'Space' has a distinct smell**: a bouquet of diesel fumes, gunpowder, and barbecue. The 'aroma' is mostly produced by dying stars.

- **An Astronomical Unit (AU)** is the average distance between Earth and the Sun, which is about 93 million miles or 150 million kilometers. Astronomical Units are used to measure distances within our Solar System.

- In the year numbering system; whether applied to the Julian or Gregorian calendars; AD 1 is preceded by 1 BC. **There is no year '0'** between them.

- If a **statue of a person on a horse** has both front legs in the air; it conveys that the person died in a battle; while if the horse has one front leg in the air; it conveys that the person died as a result of battle wounds; and if the horse has all four legs on the ground; the person died of natural causes.

- **The Sun is not a solid body,** but is composed of a gaseous plasma.

- **New York City drifts** about one inch further away from London each year.

- **The longest horns** recorded (1955) belonged to a wild water buffalo and measured 4.24 meters (13 feet 11 inches) from tip to tip.

- **Murder**, is the name for the **flock of crows**.

- Our so-called **'paper currency' is actually not made of paper.** In the USA, the Bills are made from cotton/linen material; in India, they are made with cotton and balsam; while the Euro Notes are made of pure cotton fiber.

- An Italian, **Antonio Meucci,** in 1862, **invented the first telephone**; not Alexander Bell. Bell gets the credit because he patented the invention of 'telephone' on his name later in 1876. During that 14-year period, several inventors improved on Antonio's ideas; viz., Charles Bourseul, Johann Philipp Reis, and Elisha Gray. Bell's patented telephone design used many of the improvements.

- Men who are hanged, or hang themselves, generally get **a Death Erection**, known as the 'Rigor Erectus'.

- **You won't believe why a war was suspended for two days?** In 1967, the Nigerian Civil War ground to a halt for two days because both sides wanted to watch soccer legend 'Pelé' play in an exhibition match.

- The helmets sported by the **Vikings, never had horns.**

- **Outer space is not completely empty.** It has an average density of less than one atom per cubic meter; which is very, very low. In it you can find plasma of hydrogen and helium as well as electromagnetic radiation, magnetic fields, neutrinos, dust, and cosmic rays.

- **Flamingos** can eat with their head's upside down.

- In the USA alone, medication mistakes due to the **sloppy handwriting by doctors, kills** more than 7,000 and injures 1.5 million people annually! What a shame.

- The **heaviest ball in sports** is that of 'Bowling' at 7.26 kg; while the lightest, is that of Table-Tennis at 2.7 grams.

The amazing Human Sperm.

In each ejaculation on an average, a man releases 2 to 6 milliliters of semen with up to 100 million sperms; thus theoretically, in two weeks, one man could impregnate every fertile woman on the planet.

Why are so many sperm released if it necessitates only one to construct a baby? To enter and fertilize the waiting egg, sperms in semen must travel a tough journey that only a few healthiest are able to make. Experts believe that in this way nature weeds out the weak; allowing only a healthy sperm to fertilize.

A single sperm can hold 37.5 MB worth of DNA data, and an average ejaculation can store roughly 1,500 terabytes of data.

Eight things you didn't know you could use the human semen for:

1. Soften your skin. 2. Cooking. 3. Painting. 4. Invisible ink. 5. as an antidepressant. 6. Ovulation control. 7. Aid for morning sickness. 8. Data storage.

- **All wood does not float in water**. Some will go under. There are over a dozen types of wood that are heavier than water. Water is 62.3 lbs. /ft^3 at room temperature while the heaviest wood in the world, the 'Black Ironwood' is 84.5 lbs. /ft^3 (1,355 kg/m^3).

- New Zealand was the first country that gave **women the right to vote** in national elections way back in 1893.

- The blue whale has **the largest penis** in the animal kingdom, at 8 to 10 ft. (2.4 – 3 meters) long. Its single ejaculation is about 20 liters. In the land creatures, the biggest is that of an elephant at 1.1 meters (39 in.).

- The earth has **the highest density of any planet** in the Solar System, while Saturn is the least dense of the planets.

- **Blood is always red and never blue.** The belief that bloods are blue until it touches oxygen is wrong.

- Parrots are the only birds that can **eat with** their **feet**.

- The Rotokas, the language of Bougainville, Papua New Guinea, has **the smallest alphabet** of only 12 letters. The Hawaiian language comes second with 13 letters.

- Great Albatrosses have **the largest wingspan** of any bird, exceeding 340 cm (11.2 feet).

- **Speed of light is not constant**, **it varies.** Most people will state the speed of light to be 186000 mi/s or 300000 km/s. Actually, this is the speed of light in vacuum, and taken as a constant in many areas of physics. In reality Light slows down in transparent media such as air, water, and glass.

… … … … … …

… … … … … …

… … … … … …

"The topics and the details of the facts in the various published book of facts; as well as in this small collection as an appetizer; makes one realise the infinity of the quantity of interesting facts and clarify, why such collections remain incomplete. Their incompleteness remains the main hurdle in achieving the main purpose of this book – 'To inspire, direct, and make aware".

GURU Number SEVEN

The journey from darkness to light.

The Need and the Innovation

"To be or not to be an achiever,
is not a question; because,
the diktat of never give up;
and
the spirit of survival,
are inbuilt
into the contract of everyone's life."

Our known universe has infinite interesting things. Consequently, any search of facts, even for only a single topic, is endless.

Nonetheless, I have decided to make the Facts and the Truths as the two wheels of the chariot; my book. I plan to be with them.

The mammoth monster Infinity is in front of me. Or is it all around me? Actually, I am able to see some part of it. It is not possible to comprehend how much of the monster is visible to me. I have now understood that *"When you know a little; You know; How little you know!"*

I have realized that with nothing, not even a hint to show any direction; I am not able to decide how to proceed; what to include and what not to; and where or how to go. I had set sails to explore the sea of information and am lost in its enormous size. To put it honestly, I am nowhere near finding a direction to my work. I am lost.

"This is by no means easy to accept; but then, what should I do?"

It was now time for me to introspect. "Anything which is endless cannot be completed; and I wanted to complete; how otherwise I can say I have achieved?"

I was rudderless, not knowing whether to go front, right, left, up or down; but I did understand the main question in its correct perspective and was able to orient myself to the problem.

I realized that there are various matters that can lead one into indecisiveness or depression and make the potential achiever in you, perplexed, inactive and lost. Sometimes, *'life gives us too many options'*, is one such matter, and it is affecting me now. And it is the main culprit or hurdle in my moving ahead.

"Am I approaching this task in the correct way?" I questioned myself. I was a little tense because I was going nowhere. Eventually, I acknowledged what my inner voice that said - "You need a Guru". Given the situation, my response was immediate and with a counter question: Where and how can I get the best Guru?

All of you must be wondering, as why suddenly I jumped to 'a Guru', rather than thinking about a Teacher, Professor, Coach, Preacher, Master, Guide or a Mentor?

This must be because, like many people, I also tend to think first in my mother-tongue Marathi, which, like most languages in India, have specific names for educators based on their unique abilities. And the title Guru fits exactly to the kind of educator I am looking for. And in my limited English; even though I have listed many types of educators above; there is none who exactly fits the bill. And very importantly, I want you to know what exactly I am looking for. Here is the Marathi/Sanskrit list of educators:

1) Adhyapak – Who gives information
2) Shikshak – Who informs and corrects; a disciplinary.
3) Upadhyaya – Who imparts knowledge combined with information.
4) Acharya – Who imparts skills.
5) Pandit – who is able to give deep insight in to a subject.
6) Dhrishta – Who has a visionary view and teaches you to think.
7) Guru – Who is able to awaken wisdom in you; lead you, from darkness to light.

Perhaps one needs a Guru, and maybe not. Many people call themselves 'lucky' because they have found a great Guru. There is no dearth of such people. And so, what is my difficulty? Well, there is always the opposite view of the *'other way'* thinkers. They taunt, by saying that, preachers, philosophers or religious scriptures are only needed by the weak or meek minds; thus, there is no reason to call their followers *'lucky'* about having a Guru.

When I started to look for the ablest Guru; one of the first things that struck me was that there could be a Guru in almost *everything*; very similar to the Hindu faith that *'God exists in everything'*. I also noticed that there is also a misguiding element, *'a spoiler'* in everything. My confusion increased, but I continued searching for the Best Guru for a remedy to my problem.

Searching for the greatest or best Guru, should have been easy, because many role models exist. Some are very popular, loved, and a few are even worshiped. Moses, Buddha, Jesus, Muhammad; all these great prophets are incomparable, but that's not what I am looking for.

I thought of Adi Shankara from India, Aristotle from Greece, Confucius of China and similar greats of the early civilized world. Then, the following names came up - Kant, Tennyson, Russell, Voltaire and Ruskin. *"These also won't do"*, I rationalised. I reminded myself that I am not looking for answers to questions like – *What is the significance of life?* Or *how does one attain enlightenment*? I just want to achieve successful completion of this book in the 'present' context. I accept all of them as great philosophers, but not as my Gurus for now.

I wanted a Guru that people like you and I could relate to, now, in the present situation and apt for the job in hand.

The '*present*' here is not poetic or regional; it is the present in which every form of consciousness is a reaction to a way of life that existed before, and an adaptation to new realities. This is necessary if my demonstration is to become useful to all.

"Yes, things are a little clearer to me now", I opined to pacify myself. Then an idea emerged out of the blue, '*Why don't I look up the great students? Maybe one of them or his or her guru will clear things up further*'...

One person stands out uniquely as one of the extraordinary students of all time – The legendary Mr Ekalavya. The *Mahabharata*, the great ancient epic of India, introduces Ekalavya as a young prince of a low-caste tribe. He wanted to learn Archery of the highest level. In those days it was firmly believed that any learning could not be complete and fruitful, without an educator. And here was a problem. Dronacharya, the best-known archery teacher of the time, would not accept

Ekalavya as his student because he was from a low-caste. Many from Ekalavya's village advised that it was futile for him, a low-caste, to dream of being admitted as a pupil in such privileged school. However, the boy was not put off; his determination knew no bounds.

Per epic, Ekalavya goes off into the nearby forest; where he fashions a clay image of Dronacharya; the Acharya he could not get. Worshiping the statue as his teacher, he begins a disciplined program of self-study. In time, Ekalavya becomes an archer of exceptional prowess, comparable to the best.

Moral of the story: *"I need to think out of the box, just like Ekalavya."*

My goal here is clear, but the infinite number of facts has me jammed into inaction. It might be that geniuses do not need any Guru. I am no *Socrates, William Shakespeare, Newton, Voltaire,* or *Picasso.* I am a commoner; therefore, I may need one.

My search has a definite target. I do not want to build a prophecy. Target is to be wiser, acquire required data, and find whatsoever that is missing from my arsenal to be a happy achiever. Then, let it be any Guru that helps me to meet my goal.

I began detailing this concept. "*My Guru can be like a catalyst. I must be able to love this catalyst as my*

Guru who is going to teach me how to untangle the web I am stuck in, and show me a way to reach my goal. Finally, this Guru must have something to give. Humm … this may work …"

Ekalavya found a solution in his own unique way. Likewise, I must discover or find my Guru. I want my choice of guru as an object lesson, so that all can have their own '*Guru*'. To be so universal, the choice of '*Guru*' must be simple and not representing any established doctrine.

I must think of a simpleton; which could be an abstract, as long as it is supportive of an absolutely open mind. It must also be something that everyone can find easily; an everyday thing. Simpler than the '*Cross*' or the '*Crescent of the Moon*'…

I asked myself – Why not a number as my Guru? It meets all above-mentioned conditions. By now I was so desperate, that I could accept anything and asked instantly; 'Which number should it be?'

We use numbers all the time. According to their repeated use along with a particular thing, every number gets associated with that thing. So, I must justify my choice of number.

As I began with this idea, I naturally thought of the number 'one', the popular and natural starting point. Initially, it looked right and I wrote (drew) it on paper, thanks to my architectural habit *{To remember our thoughts, we architects, Sketch or Draw, instead of writing, as it is faster}*

Soon after, it dawned on me that the number '1' is awfully similar to the letter 'I'. The 'I' that wise men have warned about, because what it represents. Many have written on the subject of the 'I'. Just listing the titles of the books on 'I' would consume dozens of pages and my book would be mistaken as one of them and get wasted.

I decided to avoid '1' and find a different number. The sooner I took this decision; by habit, I crossed the drawn numerical one.

Call it fortune, chance, fate, destiny, providence, accident, good fortune, fluke, godsend, windfall, blessing, break, kismet, opportunity, boon, or just plain luck; the '1' had become a '7' (*Seven).*

A song by the Beatles was playing on radio.
"Speaking words of wisdom, let it be... ...
Whisper words of wisdom, let it be-..."

I just let the seven (the crossed number 1) be; and made my choice – "*number seven it is,*" I said to myself.

A little later, I pondered about this choice of mine - the pick of the numeral seven. I don't have any specific use or significance of the number seven in my work as an architect, or at home as a son, husband, or parent; or even in the sports I play; at nothing. It should not really make any difference to me whichever number I choose.

I have tried to reason with myself and insist on giving other numbers a chance. Nevertheless, a mysterious fixation stops me; one that just doesn't allow me to alter my choice. The number seven holds on to the top rank with such firmness that I had begun to doubt my logic and reasonableness, and raised the following questions:

1) Why can I not like *2, 3, 4, or 5*?
2) What's my connection with seven?
3) Is the numeral seven most beautiful?
4) Do people like the number seven?
5) Do numbers have any identity?
6) Am I different?
7) What's so special about this seven?

Asking seven such questions did not help, or so it felt in the beginning. However, I did not get discouraged even though I did not get answers to the first six, because I had got wind about a key to the answer of the seventh question. This key was well-known and I spotted it.

'In God's hand is a scroll with seven seals. The author weeps when nobody is found to break the seals, ... And...... ***The number seven stands for perfection****.'* ~ the *Book of Revelation, New Testament, the Bible.'*

I may not be a Christian, but I am happy to have this revelation.

Numerology to me is akin to Astrology; unreliable. But as a man in desperation; I decided to check with Numerology; hoping to get support for my choice.

Numerologists attribute seven qualities to the number Seven: Analysis, understanding, knowledge, awareness, studious, meditating, and the seventh, 'Seeker', with no end to curiosity. This was a pleasant surprise*; 'just what the doctor ordered'*.

Well, that's it then. The 'NUMBER SEVEN' is my Guru.

Initiation

"Please be my Guru"
I Pleaded with
Sir SEVEN.

And the Number 7 replied;
so it seemed;
"Chant this Mantra seven times"
said he:

"SEVEN,
SEVEN, SEVEN,
SEVEN,
SEVEN, SEVEN,
SEVEN"

....

I realized that,
I was already chanting it aloud;
and my chanting implied that
his answer is 'yes'.

The following unfolded
after Guru Number SEVEN
accepted me as his student.

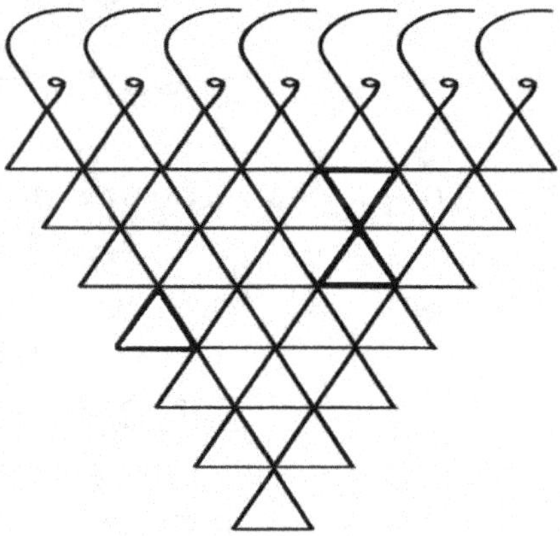

The Saraswati Yantra.

Saraswati is the Hindu goddess of knowledge, music, art, wisdom, and learning. During my days in elementary school (grades 3 to 4), to begin using each new notebook; we had to draw on the first page a 'Yantra' *representing* Goddess Saraswati (*See the opposite page)*, as a prayer for imbibing in us:

1. Curiosity and learning attitude.
2. Intense yearning (to learn).
3. Desire for obtaining guidance.
4. Perseverance and continuity.
5. Concentration.
6. Righteous and good behaviour and,
7. Sadhana - disciplined and dedicated practice or learning.

I am an atheist, but at this point, I accept that I need to imbibe these seven virtues so that I can meet my goal.

The SEVEN lines of the Saraswati Yantra represent the SEVEN virtues required of a good student. With these in my baggage, I am hopeful that Guru will accept me.

Without further delay, I drew the Yantra, and packed all seven in my baggage.

Come friends,

jump on the bandwagon.

(Do carry the Seven-Virtues pack with you)

TREASURY OF FACTS & TRUTHS

To set out with Guru Number Seven, I got a cue from the first Gurus for everyone; our mothers. And then the choice of which or whose mother was spontaneous; the common mother of all; the Mother Earth; who, by the way, gets along well with the number seven.

Due to the reflective (oceanic) water surface, the Earth is by far the brightest planet of the Solar System and a natural first choice to visit for outsiders. Although articulate earthlings call her *'the third rock from the Sun'*, for the visitors, it is the seventh major body; starting with the Kuiper Belt with its dwarf planets like Pluto as the first.

When any alien has to land here, on the earth, the traveller would have to cross seven layers of the atmosphere; just like our rockets travel through the following '*7 layers*' of the atmosphere to go into outer-space: *1. Troposphere, 2. Stratosphere, 3. Mesosphere, 4. Thermosphere, 5. Exosphere, 6. Ionosphere, and 7. Magnetosphere.* Some scientists give the following list: *1. Troposphere, 2. Ozone layer 3. Stratosphere, 4. Mesosphere, 5. Ionosphere, 6. Thermosphere, and 7. Exosphere.* Both lists are of '*seven*' layers.

Going by the Holy Qur'an, the visitor would have to cross the seven heavens. I quote: *"It is He who created everything on the earth for you and then directed His attention up to heaven and arranged it into seven regular heavens."* *(Qur'an, 2:29)*

The first for a visitor and farthest from us, the atmospheric layer '*Magnetosphere*', starts about 700 km height from the land surface and ends at about 700 miles. The *Troposphere* is the lowest layer of the atmosphere and measures about 7 miles in height and it has over 70 per cent of all the atmosphere's gases.

.... *And people question why the number seven has an 'air' about itself!*

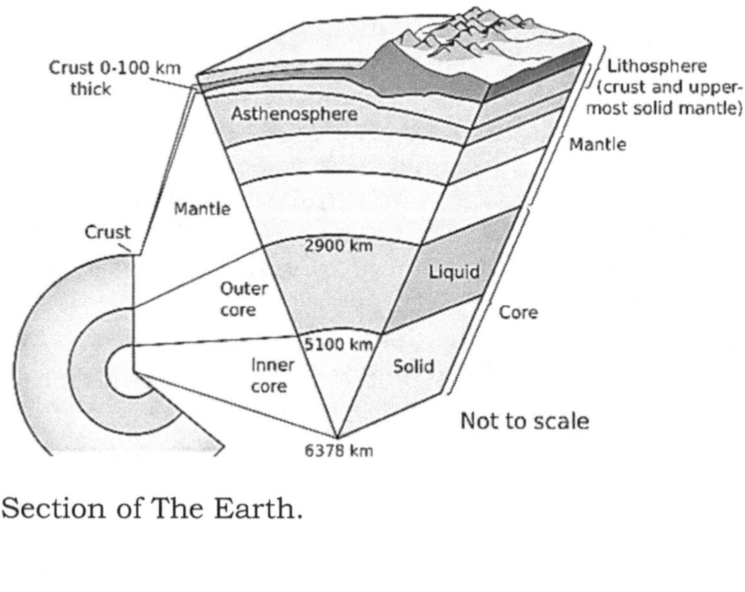

Section of The Earth.

The visitor, when he or she lands, would find that the Earth is not just a solid rock; but a living organism made up of seven distinct, successive layers. And, when the alien visitor finally reaches back '*home*', his or her report about the findings of travel would be something like this:

The aborigines call this 'Seventh Rock' in the solar system- '*Mother Earth*'. Among other things, we asked Mother Earth if she had anything to say about the number seven. This is what she answered...

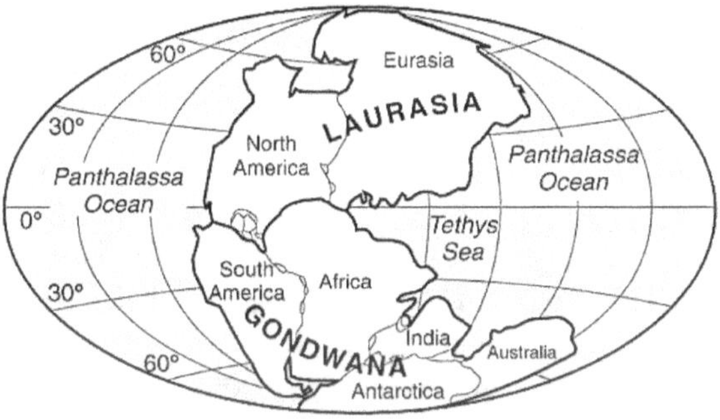

Earth about 225 million years ago,
With a single landmass called 'Pangea".

"I like my being number seven in the Solar System and I like the number seven. Why, otherwise, would I have made great effort to form the seven seas and the seven continents?" She goes on. . *"I was not born this way. It has taken a lot of time to shift the landmass to make the seas as you see them today."*

Mother Earth could not give the details of the timetable for her statement, but informed us that her humans are very good at *timekeeping*. Humans have started keeping a detailed account of the time. In this effort, the *Indian Humans* were the first to set up a detailed division of time. They had many subdivisions of the basic unit of time – the *day* - from microsecond (symbol μs), to 1 'Diwasa' (Sanskrit for - *one day*).

Ancient Indians believed that the total knowable time consists of 14 Manvantaras' (cosmic or galactic years). And of the 14 Manvantaras, the universe expands for the first Seven and contracts for the next Seven. According to them a Manvantara was about 300 million Earth years (which by modern science, is between 230 to 250 million years).

According to their calculations, the Earth was formed in the second Manvantara, while the Moon was formed in the third. Continents came out of the oceans in the fourth Manvantara. Vegetation was born in the fifth, animals in the sixth and we humans at the beginning of the current Seventh.

These divisions or subdivisions remained in the domain of the Astronomers, the Astrologers and the Physicists. It was making the week a seven-day affair; that forced the entry of the number seven into a common man's life.

A couple of billion years ago, the Sun, the earth, and the moon came to an amicable agreement about their respective everlasting timetable. It did not have anything to do with the digit seven. But then, about a few thousand years ago; we humans developed a timekeeping system called the '*calendar*'; and it has an important place for the number seven. Whether the calendar is solar or lunar, both follow a seven-day Week. Next to the day, the Week is the most important independent calendrical unit in our life. And yet, no historian has singled out the initial reason for which the Week was made of seven days. In this matter, even the skies are clueless, since nothing special happens in the sky in seven days.

The European month is obtained by division of the Solar Year by a dozen. The Islamic and Hindu month is Lunar. The months in the two systems do not coincide; nor does the beginning of the respective years. But the smaller, the seven-day Week; is exactly the same whether one follows the Solar or the Lunar calendar. We do not know exactly how this division of time began. But then, from ancient times, before the days of communication to faraway lands, Egyptians, Mesopotamians, Indians and Hebrews used the week of seven days. That all adopted a *Seven-day-week,* cannot be just a coincidence.

A long time ago, with nothing to confirm or contradict the basis of the seven-day week, an opportunist preacher spun a yarn - The legend of the Seven Day Week.

This is how it read:

"Once upon a time, in a kingdom about 7000 years ago; the people had a calendar consisting of units of year, month and day. But the Earth showed her anger unscheduled through quakes, storms, and floods. The calendar became useless. This scared everyone. Life was chaotic. A dying medicine-man told people the cause of their problems – "The Earth was unhappy. The Earth wanted a seven in the time keeping system. Till you give her the seven in timekeeping, the earth will not be calm and calamities won't stop. With nothing in the cosmos happening related to seven, I don't have an answer. But a sage with seven-inch long mustache...", and before he could go further, he died.

Nothing changed, till people heard about a sage who had a seven-inch long mustache and lived atop a tall mountain. Men and women pleaded with the sage to solve the problem. The sage went into deep meditation. People waited in anticipation. On the seventh day the sage came out of his meditation and told the people – "Go to your king. Tell him to set up a 'seven-day calendric unit called the 'Week'. Till he establishes it, the problems will continue." The great king XXX of YYY was wise and respected the sage. He set up the seven-day week to please Mother Earth. Soon enough, Mother Earth became happy and calmed down. And people lived happily thereafter."

I consider this story befitting only a fairy-tale book for children; and cannot accept it. But then, was it something like this story; however flimsy its justification might be; became a diktat. Come to think of it, life is full of such realities. As children, we all have been freely exposed to such stories. Most of us saw through their sweet lies as we grew through our teenage years. In some cases, men continue to accept them. These '*realities*' are so much a part of our lives that if you question them, society labels you a rebel or an outcast.

I do not accept any such story as factual. However, I have penned the story here because I wanted to make an example of what and why to unlearn. The unlearning here was, firstly, that the reason that the Week is of seven days is not per the fairy tale; and secondly, there is no link necessary between the Calendar of Months and the Week. Such unlearning and unlinking give a vantage that the doors that lead to reality stay open. Through such open doors I have come across a plausible logic behind the making of a seven-day week. The logic is not very feeble, and you certainly will not call it a fable.

"As man settled and special trades became a necessity. The Barter system evolved. To give effect to the trade, a scheduled periodic market became a necessity. And the schedule had to be easy to remember. With the level of communications in those days; this could be achieved only if the market day could be based on a simple calendar.

The then existing smallest calendric unit, the month, was too large or long day-group. Settlers wanted a smaller day-group. Dividing the month could not work because it brought out a fractional number and varied per the days in the month.

The wise then must have questioned – why does a calendar unit for market day be dependent on the year calendar? It can be something independent of the existing Solar or Lunar Calendar. They must have suggested - All the day unit needs to be: Of some number man could count on his fingers; Of an indivisible number for ease in counting; and of a number larger than number five.

Only one number satisfied all these requirements; the Number Seven. The Elders gave the green signal and the seven-day Week was born. In time, people all over the globe accepted the seven-day week and it continues to regulate the life of man till today."

This to me is coming closest to the logic of why the Week is of Seven days. It also clarifies why it does not relate to the Solar or the Lunar Calendar. That fifty-two of this new unit of time matches with the year, well almost; 52 X 7 = 364 is probably a coincidence.

Centuries later, the Indians named the days of the week on the planets, making it easy for people to relate to the new calendar unit. They named the days after Mars, Mercury, Jupiter, Venus, and Saturn. They had to include the Moon and the Sun to complete the seven. About the same time or with a difference of a couple of centuries the Romans also assigned names of the planets to the days of the week, almost in an identical way.

With the association of number seven and the heavenly bodies; it is not surprising that, many believed that the number seven has positive vibes, and it keeps all happy.

In continuation of this thinking, the early Hindus personified seven powers of gods, by Seven Mothers (Saptamatrika).

The Jewish tradition through the *Book of Enoch*, as if in compliance, sent only seven archangels to the seventh rock. Later, *St. John of Patmos* endorsed the number seven with his seven seals and the Orthodox continued with the seven archangels.

The Spartans and the old Persians began the education of boys at the age of *seven.* In ancient India, after reaching the age of about seven, boys left home for the residential school of a Guru.

Likewise, in early European civilizations -- with the Greeks and the Romans -- A child was not deemed responsible for any crime till he was seven, and seven was the proper age for giving a confession.

Arabic literature as well as later the Sufi showed that, traditionally love has seven stages. The seven stages are namely Hub (attraction), Uns (infatuation), Ishq (love), Akidat (trust/reverence), Ibadat (worship), Junoon (madness) and followed by Meat (death).

Nizami Ganjavi, the Persian master poet in 1197 AD, rekindled the *saga of seven* with his highly influential and famous romantic poem, '*Haft Paykar*' or '*The Seven Beauties*'. Through the seven maidens, the poem imparts seven fundamentals of culture: *Patience, Truth, Faith, Passion, Serenity, Fairness* and *Devotion to God.*

Taking a hint, artists handily adopted this number in their work; like in the instances of a casting a group of maidens as '*seven sisters*'.

Soon after establishing itself in the time system, the number seven showed how to divide the life of man into stages.

In early China, the number '7' determined the stages of female life as follows: '*a girl gets her milk teeth at seven months; loses them at seven years; reaches puberty at 2 x 7 = 14 years; and reaches menopause at 7 x 7 = 49 years.*

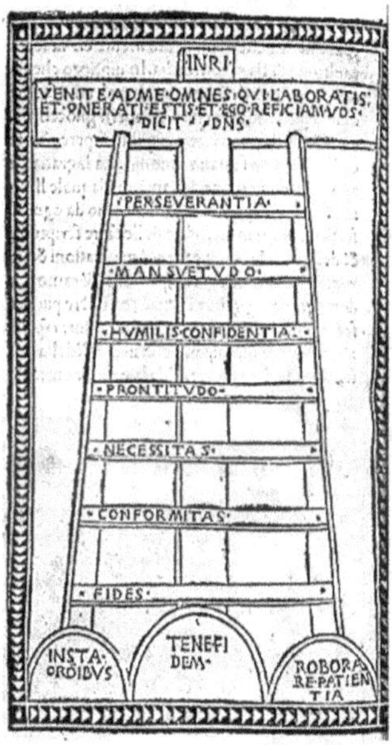

The Seven Rung Ladder of Devotion from Girolamo Savonarola's '*Epistole e diversi*', late 1497, continued the steady steps of the number seven.

After a century, William Shakespeare took up the Centre Stage. When he needed to explain the different stages of man's life, he penned a song '*The seven ages of man*', establishing continuity of the number seven in human life.

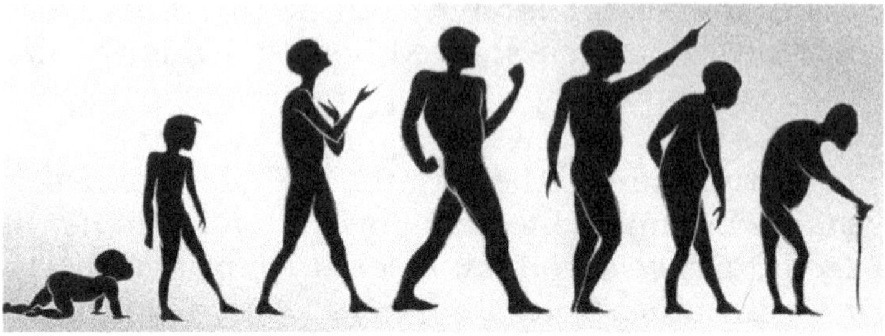

At first the infant, then a schoolboy, a lover, a soldier, the justice, lean and slipper'd Pantaloon (an aging man), and last scene of all, is second childishness and mere oblivion, Sans teeth, sans eyes, sans taste, sans everything (age of senility)."

Afterward, it was routine to divide the life in seven stages for women, namely: infant, childhood (pre-teen), the teenager, the lover, the mother, the fully retired grandma and the elderly hermit stage.

The Chinese picture here shows such seven stages.

TIME TICKS ON ... BUT,

Our present and worldwide units (divisions) of time remain seven.

The 1st Line is Seconds.

The 2nd Line is Minutes.

The 3rd Line is Hours.

The 4th Line is the Day of the Week.

The 5th Line is the Date of the Month.

The 6th Line is the Month of the Year.

And, the 7th Line is the Calendric Year.

TIME TICKS ON ... BUT,

The number seven does not simply shift from its position. And why should it?

We modern humans should have really no difficulty in accepting that numeral seven stands out boldly and positively in our life and society. We are, after all, biologically married to number Seven.

One does not need high-tech equipment to see the overwhelming connection.

The association of the human body with number seven is established much before people are born and continues to stay on till death.

Human fertilization needs involvement of Seven entities marked in the drawing below.

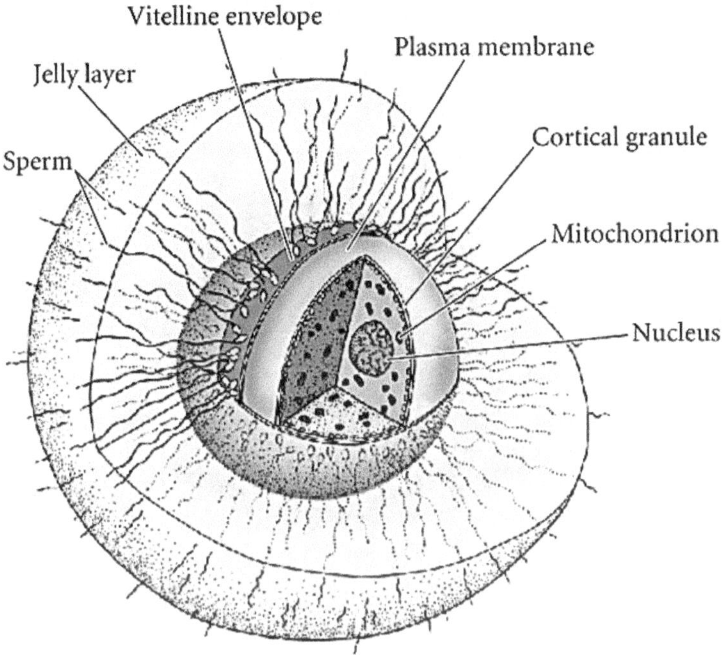

Since birth, the human **body has Seven Parts**: *head, chest, abdomen, two arms, and two legs.*

The main **internal organs** also number seven: *stomach, liver, heart, lungs, spleen and two kidneys.*

The **Bird egg** has seven parts – *Embryo, Amnion, Yolk, Allantois, Chorion, Yolk sac*, and *shell.*

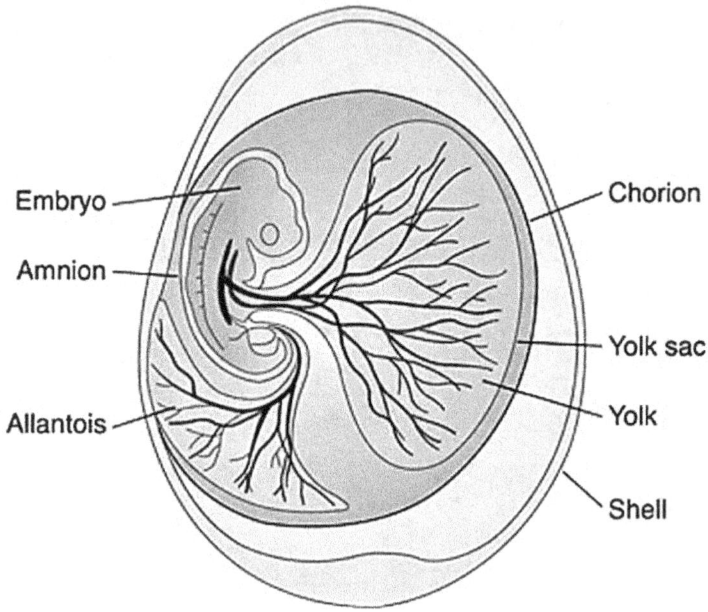

The heart has seven parts or compartments – *Aorta, Right Atrium, Left Atrium, Right Ventricle, Left Ventricle, Septum* and *Blood vessels.*

The skin has seven layers made with seven tissue systems - 1. *Stratum corneum, 2. Stratum lucidum, 3. Stratum granulosum, 4. Stratum spinosum, 5. Stratum germinativum, 6. Demis,* and *7. Subcutaneous or Hypodermis.*

The **human head** has seven windows: *two nostrils, two ears, two eyes* and *the mouth.*

The human **body functions** in seven ways: *respiration, circulation, assimilation, excretion, reproduction, sensation,* and *reaction.*

"Isn't the presence of number seven everywhere intriguing?" Wait till you see, what you see with, is made of.

The eye is made of seven main parts: *Cornea, Iris, Lens, Sclera, Retina, Macula* and *Choroid Layer.*

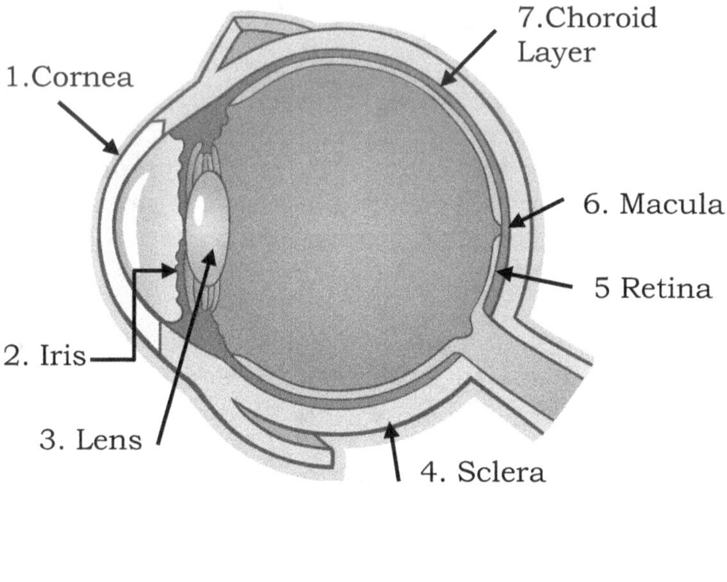

The Ear (Outer) is made up of seven Parts: *1. Canal, 2. Pinna, 3. Ossicles, 4. Drum, 5. Eustachian Tube, 6. Cochlea and 7. Auditory nerve.*

THE INNER EAR

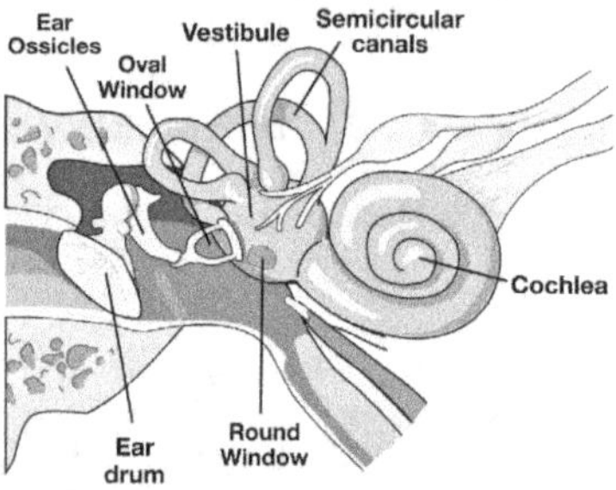

THE OUTER EAR

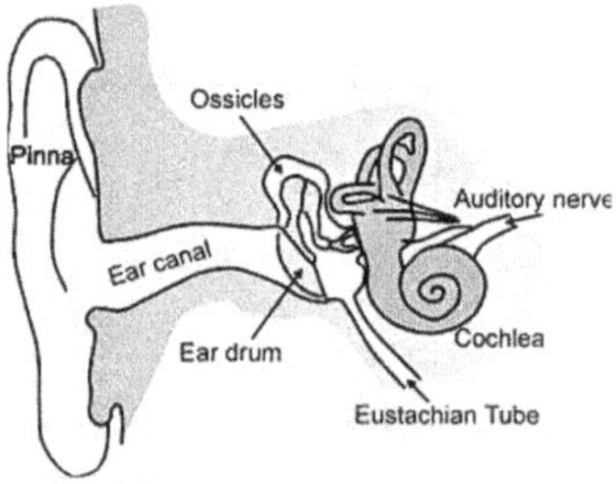

The inner ear's feelings for the number Seven run deep. It is also made up of seven parts: *1. Cochlea, 2. Round Window, 3. Drum, 4. Ossicles, 5. Oval Window, 6. Vestibule and 7. Semi-circular Canals.*

The ear respects the number seven to such an extent that when it screens all sound received; in his report to the brain; it gives good grades to only those sounds that are made from the musical pitch classes called **the seven Swaras or the seven Notes**.

*In Europe, pitch classes are typically represented by **do–re–mi–fa–sol–la–si.** However, in English- and Dutch-speaking regions, it is **A, B, C, D, E, F and G.** In Indian music, the Sanskrit names are **Sa–Re–Ga–Ma–Pa–Dha and Ni** (सा-रे-ग-म-प-ध-नि).*

All mammals have exactly **'seven' cervical Vertebrae;** no more, no less. While birds, amphibians, and reptiles have large variations in this number, in mammals it is always seven. The long necks of the giraffe and camel have seven cervical vertebrae; the same as shorter-neck humans and cats. In contrast, the long neck of the swan has 22 to 25 cervical vertebrae, and ducks have 16.

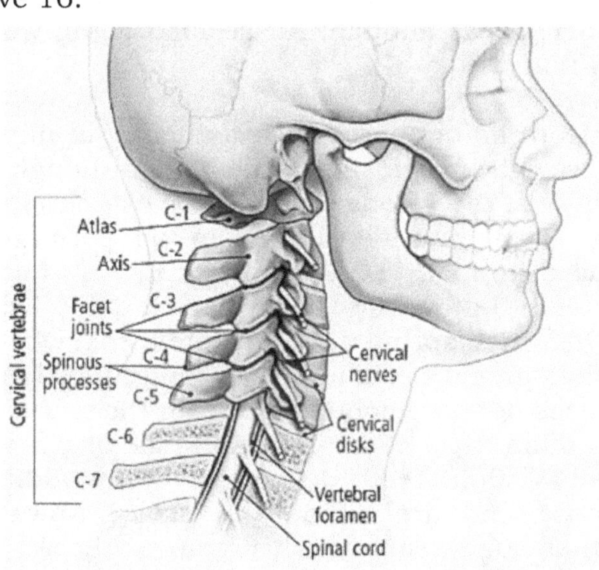

At the top of the spinal column, these bones form a flexible framework for the neck and support the head. The first cervical vertebra is the *atlas* and the second is the *axis*. The atlas' shape allows the head to nod '*yes*' and the axis' shape allows the head to shake '*no*'.

At first, **human teeth** don't seem to conform to the *dictum of seven*, as they are thirty-two in number. But if we bite into the case of the teeth, quite interestingly, the number seven comes on strong.

As the humans evolve, they need a larger skull space to accommodate a larger brain. This is achieved by reducing the size of jaw and the space for teeth. With modern cooking and diet, the smaller jaw is enough. All seemed going well for evolution.

The teeth do not agree for a reduction in number; but are fighting a losing battle here, although their enamel is the strongest and hardest part of the body. Their number is set to be permanently reduced from 32 to 28 having **four sets of seven**. The teeth that will lose their place are the '*Wisdom Teeth*', which spring up in the late teens; when the jaw has grown to its full size. The reduced size of jaw does not have enough space for them and more than often, they come in at an angle or sideways. These Wisdom Teeth do not serve any additional purpose and are difficult to clean. Nowadays, dentists unceremoniously remove these '*extra teeth*' (the Wisdoms) as soon as they give a hint of being problematic.

Evolutionists may give various reasons relating to the changes in the jaw and number of teeth, but I now pronounce that the human body wants to be faithful to the number seven very badly and that;

in future; it will have only 28 teeth in sets of sevens.

A few Ophthalmologists state that the eye has more than seven parts, but none refuses that what the eye sees is made up of seven distinct colors. The rainbow appears often enough in the sky to remind us of this fact.

From ancient times, the eyes inform that, to be beautiful all visuals must have seven fundamental qualities: *Proportion, Rhythm, Balance, Unity, Form, Harmony,* and *Familiarity.*

In time, various experts have given lists of aesthetic qualities independently; but all these lists are made up of *seven* qualities.

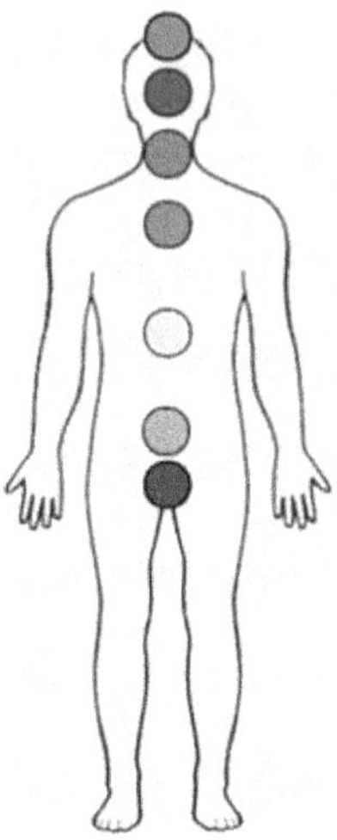

Indian spiritual science tells us that the human body has seven major energy centers; called the *Chakras.* From the bottom up:

1. Base of spine
2. Naval area
3. Near the diaphragm
4. The Heart
5. Throat area
6. Between the eyebrows
7. Top of the head.

The main fluid of the human body has not escaped the number seven. Blood is about 7% of the human body weight.

The Bones make no bones about their love for the number seven. The most common and movable joints are only seven types- Plane, Hinge, Pivot, Saddle, Ellipsoid, Universal, and Compound/Bicondyloid.

The body is helpless against harmful 'stones' forming in the body; may be because they are of seven types – 1. Bezoar in intestines, 2. Salivary in tubes carrying Saliva, 3. Gallstones in Gallbladder, 4. Tonsil Stones behind tonsils, 5. Calculus in mouth, 6. Kidney stones in Kidney, and 7. Bladder stones in the Bladder.

The number seven has man overwhelmed. He cannot get away from it even in his sleep. The US National Center for Biotechnology confirms that "people, who sleep for seven hours a night, live longest." What's more; a recent article by TNN in 'The Times of India' states that the average time a human takes to go to sleep is seven minutes.

To salute the body full of 'sevens', women wear jewellery on seven parts of the body: the head, the neck, the hands, the feet, the ears, the nose, and around the waist.

All the initial major civilizations, the Egyptian, the Mesopotamian, the Chinese and the Indian; were all formed along major and perennial rivers. There is one more thing, that is common to all. They all held number seven in high esteem. And this 'esteem' must be securely planted in the subconscious of all their people, that it remained intact, till the morning of the new prophecies.

Why, otherwise, the scriptures emerging from the locations of these civilisations rely on number seven, as if none other counted?

One cannot take the sheer consistency of the numeral seven lightly. Although, the loyalty shown by scriptures to the number seven, does not arise out of any historical fact; I notice that their saturation with the number seven, is spellbinding.

Indirectly but strongly, a hypothesis emerges that all the scriptures belong to one family; the 'family of seven'.

This hypothesis is important and should be acknowledged, especially in the context of present time, because ...

"Modern man and his media, is harping continually on 'what is different' in things to such an extent; that they have lost touch with what is not different; with what is essentially the same."

Merely to demonstrate the saturation of number seven, I would like to post a few examples here. One does not have to be a biblical scholar to see that number seven is used many many times more in the Bible than in any typical book; and, it is plainly impossible to overlook the fact.

The Old Testament uses the figure seven, seventy-seven times. Either the spirits of God are Seven, or the spirits are Sevenfold. The final book of the Bible, the Book of Revelation uses the number SEVEN all over. Everything is seven in number; churches, Spirits, Stars, Seals, Trumpets, Vials, Personages, Dooms, and what have you. Simply listing all the occurrences would take several pages.

The use of the number *seven* was very commonplace with the Aryans in ancient India. Their principal sages were seven and so were the worlds, the holy cities, the holy islands, the seas, the mountains, the forests, the sacred trees and so on. ..."

Jewish scriptures and mythology is soaked with number seven. For the ancient Hebrews, out of the many names for their gods; only seven really counted. The imperative 'Laws of Noah' are seven. The trivia in the mythology are so full of number seven that one feels someone ordered seven to be the number of everything. Dreams are also full of it; e.g. *"A Pharaoh in his dream spent seven years with each of his seven wives."*

In the Zoroastrian religion, the faith of ancient Iran, the wise lord '*Ahura Mazda*' connects with the material world through seven *emanations* or *archangels.*

Islam also loves the number seven. There are approximately twenty-five references made to the number seven in the Qur'an. These references usually concern the *seven heavens*, the *seven periods of creation*, *seven groups of things*, or *seven people* such as the *Seven Sleepers of Ephesus.* In Islam, the highest place – state of intense happiness or bliss, i.e. to be with God; is called *The Seventh Heaven.*

Buddhists cannot but love the number seven. The Buddhists took from the Aryans of India, the idea of seven stages of progressive development of the soul, and represented it by the seven storied pagodas with the umbrellas gradually reducing in size towards the top, capped with Sorin or Finial.

The mysterious Persian worship of Mithra, is full of number seven with narrations of seven gates, seven altars, and seven mysteries. Around the globe, in America, the '*Seven Sacred Rites*' form the basis of the Native American religion '*Lakota*'. Taoism works through *seven disciples* called Wang Chongyang's seven disciples.

Atheists may spurn the concept of God, but they have not been able to circumvent the use of number seven. Atheist Dr Karenga's hatred of God-fearing religions prompted him to create his own scheme of principles called 'Kwanzaa'. The core principles of Kwanzaa are *Seven.*

This bond with the numeral seven also holds true with the Early Christian Gnostics, the collectors of ancient religious ideas and systems which originated in the first century AD among early Christian and Jewish sects. They state that every planet must support seven major races of mankind, called the Root-Races. Many theosophists cling to the number seven and explain: There are seven Root-Races, or evolutionary cycles through which humanity evolves. Each root-race is divided into seven minor cycles called sub-races, which are again subdivided into seven branch or family races.

With such high spiritual support to the number seven, the spirits of my Guru are on the seventh high! He goes on to point out that, although religions seem different, they all are singing the *same song...* The song of number seven!

The dance of the spiritual rituals is not different from the scriptures. In an equally noticeable way, the rituals cling to the number seven. The rituals of faraway lands collectively continue to convey, through the simple common symbol of the number seven, that *all heartbeats have the same rhythm.*

The most sacred rituals of Christian faith are the *Seven Sacraments.* The first 4 sacraments are about the life of Christ. These are *Baptism, Penance, Ordination* and *Eucharist.* The remaining three are, *Marriage, Extreme Unction,* and Confirmation.

On their pilgrimage to Mecca, Muslims go around Kaaba *seven* times. Circling around the Kaaba represents the idea of *oneness* and trying to uplift people to a higher level. Each turning round the Kaaba represents the ascent from the lower step of the psyche, to the higher.

The Hindu's believe that a soul has seven successive human lives. This '*seven*' is registered so deeply with the women of India that in their yearly ritual for everlasting relationship of marriage; they go around a tree seven times and pray for getting a husband with the same soul for all the remaining out of his seven lives.

In Hindu weddings, the most important rite is the Saptapadi (*Seven Steps*) or (*seven*) Phere (*going around the holy fire*). Here the bride and the bridegroom take *seven steps* together or go around the nuptial fire seven times and make *seven promises* to each other. Like every ritual in India, the details of ceremonies vary in different regions. The text is also changed in some places; but the number seven remains unchanged.

Among the Hebrews, every seventh year is a sabbatical year, and seven times seven years is the jubilee. There are 7 holidays in the Jewish year. In the weekly reading, the scriptures are divided into seven portions for seven men to read simultaneously. During a Jewish wedding ceremony, the priests recite seven blessings and the bride circles the groom 7 times. In Judaism, the period of prescribed mourning that begins immediately after the burial, lasts seven days. The name for this mourning period is *Shivah* (*in Hebrew for seven*).

The Egyptians had *seven* original and higher gods. The Persians believed in the *seven sacred horses of Mithra*; while their countrymen the Zoroastrian Parsees, hold that the *seven angels are opposed by seven demons*.

In the Middle Ages an oath had to be taken before seven witnesses, and the one, to whom it was administered, was sprinkled seven times with blood. The processions around the temples went *seven* times, and the devotees had to kneel *seven* times before uttering a vow.

The idea of the '*seven Souls*' is found with both, the early Egyptians and the Hindus of Vedic period. The following table shows the similarities:

INDIAN	SOUL	EGYPTIAN
Rupa, or form of body	1	*Kha,* body
Prana, or the breath of life	2	*Ba,* the soul of breath
Astral body	3	*Khabas,* the shade
Manus or intelligence	4	*Akhgu,* Intelligence or perception
Khama-Rupa or animal soul	5	*Seb,* Astral soul
Buddhi or spiritual soul	6	*Putah,* the first intelligent father
Atma, pure spirit	7	*Atmu,* divine, eternal soul

For the New Year, Irani families spread a ceremonial cover onto the dining table and serve *seven dishes called 'Haft-Sin': sprouted wheat, apples, pudding, dried fruits, garlic, wild rue* and *vinegar.*

Moses used a seven-branch lamp stand, the Menorah, to set up the portable sanctuary in the wilderness and later in the temple in Jerusalem. The menorah has now become one of the symbols of Judaism.

Post renaissance, drawing seven sided patterns, like the one here, became a hobby with artists.

Seven is a traveller par excellence. Seven is everywhere; and everywhere it is at home. Its ability to listen to new cultures; the ease with which it blends in and be a useful friend; have earned it the *citizenship* everywhere it has gone.

Let us travel around to meet the balance fan clubs...

Before we begin to travel; let me appraise you that there are Seven Things that money cannot buy; anywhere on the Earth.

1. True Love
2. Passion
3. Time
4. A happy family
5. Knowledge
6. Respect, and
7. Inner peace.

An Egyptian math quiz found on Papyrus.
(about 1650 BC)

"As I was going to St Ives,
met a man with seven wives,
each wife had seven sacks,
each sack had seven cats,
each cat had seven kits:
kits, cats, sacks and wives,
How many were going to St Ives?"

That the Egyptians considered that the number seven was special is obvious from the fact that for maximum security; they had *seven doors* with *seven shutters* to protect their holiest.

In order that the offering to the Gods was full, they used a *seven chambered* tablet. The number seven was the Egyptian symbol of perfection, effectiveness, and completeness.

Ancient Egyptians considered *Seven Oils* as Sacred for their powerful stimulating effects. They are Spikenard (*physical powers*), Olibanum (*sense of smell*), Palm (*energy*), Myrrh (*blood*), Juniper (*calm and cleanse*), Fo-ti-Tieng, (*sexual*), and Lotus, (*the sweetness of a woman*).

The Chinese love the number seven. In Chinese culture, the number seven features rather prominently in many aspects of life. For example, the seventh day of the first moon of the lunar year is known as *Human's Day.* For the Chinese that day is the birthday of all human beings universally. That is why a Chinese person is a year older on that day, regardless of what his or her actual date of birth is. This is not to say that the Chinese don't celebrate a birthday on the *real day* of birth; they most certainly do. When it comes to a death, the Chinese hold a special ceremony on the 49th day after death; that is, *7 X 7 days.* It means the final farewell.

The Chinese celebrate Valentine's Day on the 7th day of the 7th lunar month in the Chinese calendar. There is an interesting love story behind this day. The 7th daughter of the Emperor of Heaven and an orphaned cowherd were in love and wanted to marry. The Emperor played spoilsport and separated both of them. He moved the 7th daughter to the star called *Vega* and the cowherd to the star named *Altair.* They can meet only once a year - on the *7th day of the 7th lunar month.*

The Buddhists of Japan believe in seven reincarnations. According to Japanese mythology, the world begins with the birth of seven deities. These seven deities arise and then pass away in what the Japanese call '*the plain of high heaven*'. There are *seven* basic principles of the *Bushido*, the code of honor and morals for Samurai warriors.

The *seven* are: *justice or rectitude, courage, benevolence or mercy, respect, honesty, honour,* and *loyalty.*

The Japanese *Tanabata* festivities begin on the 7th day of the 7th month, the 7th July. This festival originates from a Chinese festival mentioned earlier.

The Japanese celebrate a baby's birth on the 7th day. They mourn a death for *seven* days and again, after *seven* weeks. On the 7th day of the year, the Japanese eat seven-herb rice porridge *(nanakusa)* for health and happiness.

Tibetans believe that seven great rays exist in the cosmos as the channels through which all beings in the solar system flow - the seven main characteristics or changes of life. The Tibetan Master, Djwhal Kuhl *says* ≈ *"For it is not to humanity alone that these rays apply; but to the seven kingdoms as well. In fact, there is nothing in the solar system, at whatever stage of evolution it may stand, which does not belong and has not always belonged to, one or other of the seven rays".*

In Eastern Europe, in making up for a quarrel or signing a treaty of peace, the rulers exchanged either *seven* or forty-nine (*7 X 7*) presents.

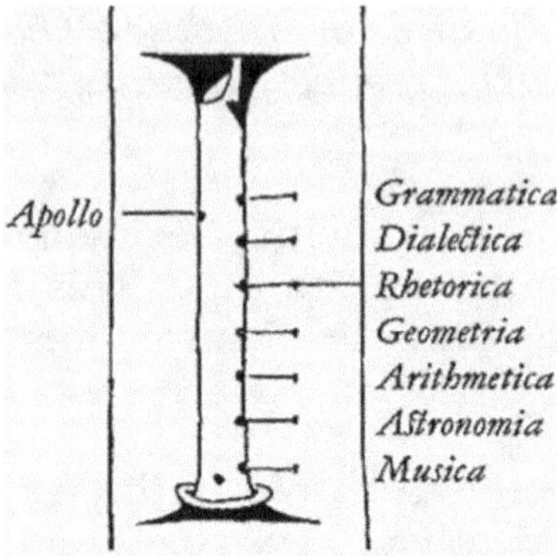

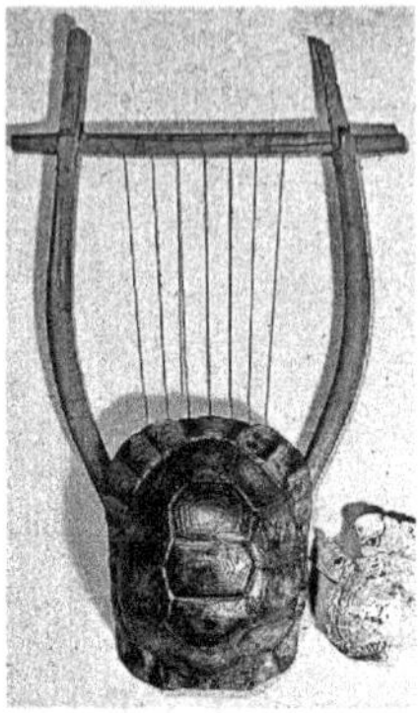

The Greeks show their love for the number seven through their best-loved Sun god *Apollo,* who brings life-giving heat and light to Earth. For such a '*God*' the Greeks held seven chief Apollonian festivals. The Logic of seven is obvious; after all, Apollo was the 7-faced pillar of all knowledge and he is often depicted carrying a lyre, the beloved Greek musical instrument with *seven strings...*

The Seven Sages of Greece (620 BC – 550 BC), was primarily the title given by Ancient Greek tradition to the seven wise men of distinction. The Greek legend '*Seven against Thebes*', has seven heroes who made war on *Eteocles*, the king of Thebes.

Germans embrace the number seven as the *number of the justice*. According to them a place must have *seven* trees to hold the old German tribunals. Seven judges seated under the trees required *seven* witnesses for giving a verdict. Early Germans placed great importance on the *seventh* son of a *seventh* son. All German mythic personages are generally endowed with *seven* sons. In Germany, even the king could not refuse to stand as the godfather to a *seventh* son, *even if he were a son of a beggar.*

Hindu mythology travelled east and along with it, travelled many ideas. The temple of Phnom Bakheng, the Center of the first kingdom of Angkor, has seven levels (*ground, five tiers, and upper terrace*) representing the seven heavens of '*Indra*' (*the king of the Gods*).

The Thai, call the Pleiades as the 'Dao Look Kai' or the Seven Chicks. The story behind this naming is: God gave seven chicks a rebirth and placed them in the sky because the seven chicks who loved their mother so much that they threw themselves on the fire, where someone was cooking their mother for a meal.

The Seven-Headed Naga serpents depicted as statues in Cambodian temples, such as Angkor Vat, apparently represent the 7 races within Naga society.

'Naga' is a Sanskrit name for snake *Cobra.* This serpent has been associated with many mythological beliefs in India since time immemorial.

The Thai also believe in the seven headed Naga; but here I believe, it is because of the influence of Hindu mythology; rather than the Naga society.

Long before Columbus reached America; the number seven reached the Easter Islands off Chile in the South-eastern Pacific Ocean. The islands are one of the most remote inhabited islands in the world, with nearest inhabited land over 2000 km away.

During the 13th and 14th century, Rapa Nui people of the Eastern Island carved huge human figures, called the Moai. Some are 30 feet tall and weighing 80 tonnes. The Moai sculptures are remarkably creative and physical feats by any measure.

These seven Moai in the picture are pretty intense. They are the only ones to face outwards towards the ocean, in the fairly accurate direction of Tahiti, where the people came from.

"The fact that the Earth comprises seven layers is now established. Physiologists have found that human skin has seven layers. Anatomists confirm that the heart has seven chambers. These facts together, point out that it is plausible, that only one system governs all the creation in the universe.

No wonder Einstein pondered over the idea of a seven-dimensional universe!!!" ...

Einstein and all Physicists attach great importance to seven. And why would they not? Atoms have seven shells. Each atom consists of a nucleus (composed of protons and neutrons) and seven shells of electrons. The shells are paths where the negative charged electrons orbit the nucleus in an elliptical way. With more energy the electron jumps to higher and higher shells, until it reaches the uppermost seventh level.

The total energy of a system can be subdivided and classified into potential energy, kinetic energy, or combinations of the two in various ways. But, the most applicable and therefore named forms of energy are seven: 1. Chemical, 2. Potential, 3. Nuclear, 4. Kinetic, 5. Heat, 6. Radiant and 7. Sound.

Chemistry is immensely partial to the number 7. Seven is the atomic number of Nitrogen; by far the largest component of the Earth's atmosphere.

A chemical solution having an exact pH of 7.0, is 'neutral'; meaning neither acidic nor alkaline. Only pure water has the exact pH value of seven and is truly neutral. Distilled water, and rain water, commonly believed to be pure; tend to be slightly acidic.

Botany bags the beans with all the trees being made of seven elements: *1. Seed, 2. Root, 3. Trunk (bark), 4. Branch-structure, 5. Leaves, 6. Flowers,* and *7. Fruits.*

Geometry is far in advance of its rivals in its connectedness with the figure seven.. This old Egyptian geometric archetype is a cryptic symbolization of the number seven. The seven turns, *3+4 left-right turns* -- represent man and woman.

John Dee, the advisor to the English Queen Elizabeth I, created a '*Seal*' with an uncommon seven-sided geometric shape. *Seven-sided,* because only angels could divide a circle into seven equal parts; something that was beyond the capacity of common man.

The Pythagoreans regarded the number seven as perfect, because it is made up of three plus four; representing a triangle and a square. For them, that circle cannot be divided into seven parts by any known geometrical construction; was enough to call it a mystic number.

Theosophists, who believe in the sevenfold universe, consider the number seven a very important number. They say, "This numerical key of the number seven lies at the root of all evolution, whether physical or spiritual. It is the key which unfolds all mysteries of nature."

There are seven Arts of Power: 'Literature', 'Performing Art', 'Visual Art', 'Design Art', 'Decorative Art', 'Technological Art', and 'Religion'.

Architecture has always loved the number seven. Ruskin, in his famous treatise on Architecture, declared that the guiding 'lamps of architecture' are Seven: Beauty, life, memory, obedience, power, sacrifice, and truth.

Sumerian Borsippa Ziggurat, now in Iraq, was laid out in seven terraces and reached a height of more than 70 meters in ancient times.

Athena, Athene, or 'Athena the Virgin', is an ancient Greek goddess associated with wisdom, handicraft, and warfare. Seven was her number since it is a virgin number (a prime number).

It is befitting that one of the greatest architectural masterpieces, the 'Parthenon', is the temple of the goddess Athene. Due to its immense presence; that its inviting entrance of the majestic colonnade has seven bays on the front side; sometimes goes unnoticed.

The primary scale of architecture relates to the size of the human body and its reach. The height of an average man with raised hands is *seven feet.* If man spreads his arms sideways without moving his feet, the horizontal area of reach is again seven feet. This is the reason that architects prescribe seven feet as the height of the common doors.

S*even* gigantic walls enclose the Sri Ranganathaswami Temple, forming seven courts or Prakaras within them. The island-town of Srirangam, India, spread over 600 acres. The total length of these seven walls is about *seven* miles. The temple complex has (*7x 3*) 21 ornate Gopurams (monumental towers); at the entrance of each temple.

Most of the loved cities have a strong connection to the number seven. Mumbai (*Bombay*) connected seven islands into one to become what it is.

The abode of Lord Venkateshwara, the richest temple in the world, in the town of Tirupati, spreads over seven hills. Rome is also built on seven hills named - *1. Aventine, 2. Palatine, 3. Capitoline, 4. Caelian, 5. Quirinal, 6. Viminal, and 7. Esquiline.*

'Wikipedia' and 'answers.com' list the cities that are built on seven hills. Starting from Jerusalem, Pretoria, Kampala, Rio de Janeiro, Cincinnati-Ohio, Richmond-Virginia, Tokyo, Seattle-Washington, Washington-DC, San Francisco, Amman, Istanbul, Brussels, Prague, Bath, Bristol, Cambridge, Athens, Lisbon, Moscow, Istanbul, Brisbane, and Melbourne.

All are popular and important. Is this because they are connected to the number seven?

According to an Arabian legend; seven angels cool the sun with ice and snow, lest it should burn the earth to cinders; and seven thousand angels wind up and set the sun into motion every morning.

The Law is, above all, they say; but it is not above the number seven. Advocacy must adhere to its seven lamps: *1) Honesty, 2) Courage, 3) Industry, 4) Wit, 5) Eloquence 6) Judgment, and 7) Fellowship.*

… … … … … …

… … … … … …

… … … … … …

With the first successful human spaceflight Apollo 7; number seven raised its globe-trotting limits to new heights. We shall certainly benefit from Guru's ability of having a 'satellite view' of things; in addition to the 'worms eye view' and the 'birds eye view'.

"I have a thing about coincidences.

The word **heaven**,

bears a strong phonetic resemblance

to the word **seven**.

I marvel,

whether the noun **seven,**

paved the way for the noun **heaven**;

Or... is it the other way round?...

Irrespective of the similarity in the names; the heavens like the number seven. Many constellations have seven bright stars. The most prominent are the Great Bear and the Pleiades.

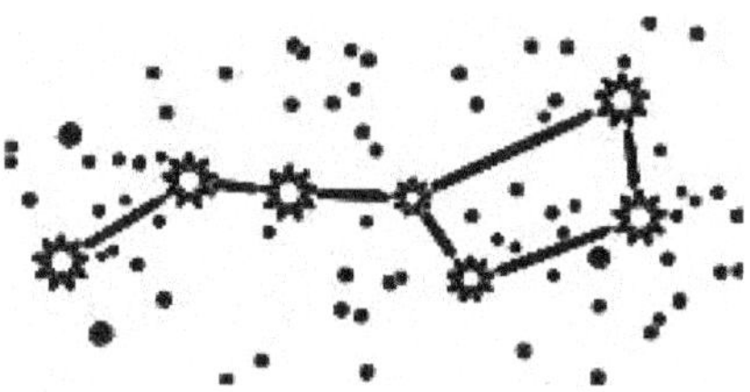

The Great Bear or the Ursa-major is *'Saptarishi'* in India, where the seven stars get their names after the seven sages.

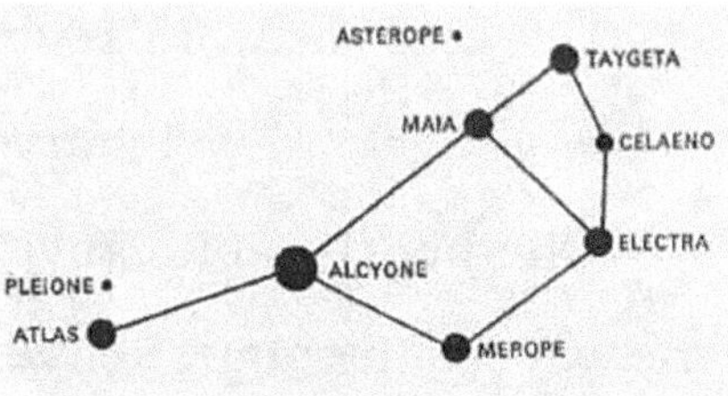

The Pleiades, the seven daughters of Atlas are known as the seven sisters by many cultures; and in Thailand as the Seven Chucks.

Exactly like the adherence to the number seven by rituals in several regions of the world; almost all the enlightened Gurus, Prophets, Psychologists and Philosophers, divide their message into seven chapters or statements. Like the *'Buddhist Seven Steps to Nirvana.'*

Aristotle (384-322 BC), the Greek philosopher, is probably the first on record for *'a law of seven'* - *"Every action is due to one or other of seven causes: chance, nature, compulsion, habit, reasoning, anger, or appetite."*

Almost all preachers point out that principal *Virtues* are '*Seven*'; *1) faith, 2) prudence, 3) hope, 4) charity, 5) justice, 6) fortitude* and *7) temperance.*

Swami Chinmayananda from India says, *"From 'him' are born Seven Pranas (life sources or breaths), the seven flames, sevenfold fuel, the sevenfold oblations, as also seven worlds where Pranas move into the cave of living creatures; seven and seven."* ... (*Mundakopanisad - 8th verse*)

The most important of writings by *Longchenpa*, the Tibetan Buddhist Guru, are '*The Seven Treasuries*':

1. Treasury of Philosophy (g*rub mtha' mdzod*)
2. Treasury of the Sublime Vehicle (t*heg mchog mdzod*)
3. Treasury of Wish fulfillment (*Yid bzhin mdzod*)
4. Treasury of Secret Instructions (*man ngag mdzod*)
5. Treasury of the Dharmadhatu (*chos dbyings mdzod*)
6. Treasury of the Natural State (*gnas lugs mdzod*)
7. Treasury of Word and Meaning (*tshig don mdzod*)

We can see the love for the number seven in the works of Greek-Armenian sage *Gurdjieff.* Gurdjieff talked of a '*law of seven*'. His law had seven intervals in it.

Revered Yoga Guru Prof. Iyengar invoked seven mothers in his Saga; the seven invoked are *Devahuti, Sukanya, Devayani, Damayanti, Renuka, Draupadi and Kannaki.*

The foremost qualities of a wise person are also '*Seven*' - *Comprehensiveness, Sensibility, Selectivity, Objectivity, Openness, Consistency* and *Decisiveness.*

The fundamental teachings of the Holy '*Bhagwat Gita*' are '*seven*': *1. Know the reality of the cosmos where you exist. 2. Experience the Reality about yourself. 3. Recognize that the senses are responsible for your desires. 4. Cultivate your discriminating intelligence to discern true knowledge. 5. Understand the true nature of action and inaction. 6. Know the Supreme-Self; the all-pervading and all-knowing Creator of all. 7. Cultivate quality of 'Sattva' or purity.*

While some of the above is not easy to understand; 'The seven treasures' by Dr Mark Keaveny, are not difficult at all. They are: 1. Gathering of friends 2. Strategic-Problem-solving. 3. Teamwork. 4. Creativity. 5. Role-playing. 6. Spontaneity. 7. Mystic storytelling.

'The Number Seven' itself does not worry about the number it represents, nor of its universal appeal. But yet, as we have witnessed; it scores positively with many. And with the 'spirituals', the number seven scores a 'perfect ten'.

Who else does the number seven score brownie points with? Let's go find out, shall we? ...

Seven' may not be a magical number, but it does have an uncanny knack of appearing in all sorts of situations. The remarkable part is that this quality associated with the number seven; is consistent throughout civilizations.

The march of the number seven continues from the Seals of the Indus valley; through the conclusion that principal metals are seven; and the finding that the number 7 is the atomic number of 'Nitrogen'; whose quantity is estimated at about seventh of the total mass in the Milky Way and the Solar System.

And that the computer network is best understood in seven layers, ...

Curiosity and necessities of the nomad man presented him agriculture and in turn led him into creating settlements. But curiosity got the better of the comfort of that very settlement and made him step out and look around. He recognized that he belonged to a large global community, and as such, he searched all over to locate the great achievements of his fellow men in the whole universe. As he travelled far and wide, he did come across some extraordinary accomplishments.

It would not have interested me at this time or have any reference to this writing, if the traveller had called anyone/anything the greatest or best. However, he did not do so. He chose to empanel a few great creations, and named them as the wonders of the universe. Different people have put forward many lists of 'wonders of the world' in their time and depending on their exposure and interest of topics; however, all have one thing in common – all lists are of seven things, seven buildings or seven items. And this is why I have to include these in this discussion.

I was not surprised to see a heading in the local newspaper a decade back saying, 'The world is awaiting the new Seven Wonders of the World. The news was that a Swiss Organization was in the process of re-scrutinizing and naming the best wonders. New lists will keep on coming. Let us enjoy some of the important ones...

The first list was 'The Seven Wonders of the Ancient World'; given by Diodorus Siculus and Antipater of Sidon; both lived before 100 BC. 1. The Lighthouse of Alexandria, 2. The Colossus of Rhodes, 3. The Hanging Gardens of Babylon, 4. The Temple of Artemis at Ephesus, 5. The Statue of Zeus at Olympia, 6. The Mausoleum at Halicarnassus, and the only survivor - 7. The Great Pyramid of Giza. These creations rivalled many created by nature in their size, majesty, and beauty. Six of the seven wonders can no longer be seen; having been destroyed by natural disaster or by men. Let us see what they 'really' were.

The Lighthouse of Alexandria.

The Lighthouse of Alexandria, sometimes called the Pharos of Alexandria was a lighthouse constructed by the Ptolemaic Kingdom, during the reign Ptolemy II Philadelphus (280–247 BC). One estimate states its overall height to be 100 meters (330 ft). It had to be repaired Many times, does not speak of high-quality construction. An earthquake damaged it beyond repairs and finally it was abandoned as a ruin.

It was referred to as the tallest man-made structure. But it was not. The 139 meters tall Pyramid at Giza, was.

The Colossus of Rhodes.

The Colossus of Rhodes was a statue of the Greek sun-god Helios. It was erected in Rhodes city, on the Greek island of the same name, by Chares of Lindos in 280 BC. According to most contemporary descriptions, the Colossus stood about 33 meters (108 feet) high—the approximate height of the modern Statue of Liberty from feet to crown—making it the tallest statue of the ancient world. It held out just over 50 years and collapsed during the earthquake of 226 BC. Some mystery remains as to where it was really located and what happened after it collapsed. What we know is that even if it did exist, it was never rebuilt.

The Statue of Zeus.

The Statue of Zeus at Olympia was a giant seated figure, about 13 m (43 ft) tall, made by the Greek sculptor Phidias around 435 BC at the sanctuary of Olympia, Greece. It was lost and destroyed during the 5th century AD. Nothing about it has been actually found; and details of its form etc., are known only from ancient Greek descriptions and representations on coins.

Zeus sat in the temple at Olympia and presided over the (Olympic) Games until AD 392; after which, in a couple of years, the Christian Emperor of Rome, Theodosius I, abolished the Games as he considered them pagan or irreligious.

The Hanging Gardens of Babylon.

Owing to the lack of documentation in coexistent Babylonian sources; it is not clear whether the 'Hanging Gardens' were an actual construction or a poetic creation. To date, no archaeological evidence has been found at Babylon or anywhere else about the Hanging Gardens.

The Temple of Artemis.

The Temple of Artemis was located near the ancient city of Ephesus, in Turkey. It was a Greek temple dedicated to an ancient, local form of the goddess Artemis. The temple was built by Croesus, king of Lydia, about 550 BCE and was rebuilt after being burned by a madman named Herostratus in 356 BC. The temple was destroyed by invading Goths in 262 CE and was never rebuilt. It was the largest floor area single temple in the then known world. Size: over 350 by 180 feet (about 110 by 55 metres). But one cannot be sure about its design and beauty. Opinions differ about the design of the temple of Artemis. Some say the 'Order' of its columns was Ionic, while some say it was Corinthian, and some say the columns belonged to none of the 'orders'. See the images below claiming to be the Artemis Temple.

The Greek authors who wrote the first list of the Seven Wonders of the World, belonged to the 2nd Century BC. They must have known the rebuilt Acropolis Complex (460 - 430 BC) which had a much larger area than the Temple of Artemis, and more importantly it included the Parthenon, and the Propylaea (monumental gateway). That makes the choice of Temple of Artemis in the list of seven, a wonder in itself.

The Mausoleum at Halicarnassus.

The Mausoleum at Halicarnassus was a tomb built between 353 and 350 BC in Bodrum, Turkey, then part of the Persian Empire. The Mausoleum was about 45 m (148 ft.) in height, and sculptural reliefs adorned its four sides. Out of the six 'wonders' that do not exist, the tomb lasted longest; till about the 12th century AD.

The Great Pyramid of Giza.

The Lone survivor out of the seven. With material of construction similar to the other wonders; why only the Pyramid at Giza still stands proud?

It is because of its form. This form, brings the center of gravity closer to the ground and its very wide base removing any possibility of toppling even with sever side pressures. Additionally, the angle of the taper of sides is lowered to about 51^0, which eliminates the slumping action.

As the memories of ancient wonders faded and man built new fascinating things, some items were gradually expelled from the list of wonders and were replaced by other achievements.

Middle-Age thinkers, selected following as the wonders:

Stonehenge (UK - 3000 BC to 2000 BC), The Colosseum (Rome – AD80), The Catacombs of Kom el Shoqafa (Alexandria, Egypt – 2nd Century AD), The Great Wall of China (700 BC to 200 BC), The Porcelain Tower (China –15th Century AD), The Hagia Sophia (Istanbul - AD 537), The Leaning Tower of Pisa (Italy 12th Century AD).

I find it noteworthy that the new list of the seven wonders of the Middle-Ages, removed all wonders listed earlier. One can understand that the persons who chose seven wonders of the Middle-Ages did not believe in the *six* that could no longer be seen; but I fail to understand the removal of the pyramid from the list of wonders and at the same time inclusion of 'Stonehenge UK'.

Two things are misfit here. Firstly; how come a structure built-in the 15th Century AD found a spot in the list of wonders of the High Middle ages? Secondly, how come the list does not find a place for the 'Kailas Rock-cut temple' of Ellora, India (7th Century AD)?

The Kailash Temple at Ellora is the largest monolithic structure in the world, carved top-down from a single rock. The scale at which the work was undertaken is enormous. Compared to Parthenon in Athens, it covers twice the area and is 1.5 times higher. It meant cutting and taking out a whopping 200,000 tonnes of rock. It took 7,000 laborers 150 years to finish the task.

Among the achievements of man; the *Leaning Tower of Pisa,* a blunder, finds a pride of place in the list of great wonders. It is amazing that the tower has survived; however, I find its appreciation shocking. I wonder whether, *'As an architect, can I go scot-free if any structure of mine 'tilts'?'*

No one has identified the authority that published these lists, and who it was, that gave them that authority. Who determined that all lists must number seven? Still, they exist and most men and women accept them.

The Seven Wonders of the Industrial World followed in time. *'SS Great Eastern',* the big iron ship capable of carrying 4000 passengers non-stop from England to Australia, *'The Bell Rock Lighthouse', 'The Brooklyn Bridge'* (one of *the first cable-stayed/ suspension bridge*), *'The London Sewers', 'The transcontinental railroad', 'the Panama Canal'* and *'The Hoover dam'.*

Geography also whispers its choice of seven wonders as *'the seven natural wonders of the world'* excluding *'the seven seas and seven continents'*. The list goes as follows: *1. Mount Everest, 2. The Matterhorn, 3. The Meteor Crater, 4. Victoria Falls, 5. Ayers Rock, 6. The Grand Canyon,* and *7. The Great Barrier Reef.*

I cannot place all such lists of wonders here. They are easy to find. Let me stop with the Seven Wonders of the Modern World: The Empire State Building, The Itaipu Dam, The CN Tower, The Panama Canal, The Channel rail Tunnel, North Sea protection works, The Golden Gate Bridge.

The list of wonders being of only seven things; the number seems to validate them as something supreme and incomparable; as if nothing else is or was as wonderful.

Walking down a road numbered *'seven'* is educative as you recognize that *seven* is the number of the 'true' wonders which are timeless truths. No one needs to travel far to find them.

The *SEVEN* human abilities are the true wonders. 1. *To smell 2. To See, 3. To hear, 4. To Touch, 5. To Taste, 6. To Feel, & 7. To Love.*

We can use these abilities because we are *alive*. We have a *life*. Anything purported to have *'life'* must have seven qualities or qualifications.
The seven qualifications of life are:

1. Movement (plants don't walk across the garden, but they do move in various ways).
2. Feeding (Plants draw food from roots; some eat insects and augment it using photosynthesis).
3. Growth.
4. Take in and get rid of gases.
5. Sensitivity. (Responding to surroundings)
6. Reproduction.
7. Excretion or getting rid of waste.

If you are looking for qualities or traits, instead of qualifications, Biology again turns to its beloved seven; and gets it confirmed that having the following seven qualities should be enough for accepting the presence of life.

1. Homeostasis: Regulation of internal environment.
2. Organization: structurally composed of cells.
3. Metabolism: Transformation of energy and decomposing organic matter.
4. Growth: Increasing size of all its parts.
5. Adaptation: Ability to change in response to the environment.
6. Response to stimuli.
7. Reproduction: Ability to produce new individual organisms.

"From wonders to the wonderful; the way the number seven dwells everywhere, is really wonderful."

The treasurers of yesteryear name only *Seven as Treasures*: *Gold, Silver, Lapis Lazuli (the deep blue stone), Crystal, Agate, Red Pearl* and *Carnelian*. They also name only seven as powers: *faith, perseverance, sense of shame, avoidance of wrongdoing, mindfulness, concentration* and *wisdom.*

The East in antiquity, had named *seven* principal rivers *(the Nile, the Tigris, the Euphrates, the Oxus, the Yaksart, the Arax and the Indus).*

Musical instruments are of seven types:
1. *Wind instruments, 2. Lamella phones, 3. Percussion instruments, 4. String instruments, 5. Electronic instruments, 6. Keyboard instruments,* and *7. Voice.*

Transport types we now use are seven: *1. Human – self-carrying, 2. With the use of Human energy – cycle, 3. With the use of animal energy – bullock cart, horse wagon, 4. Shipping, 5. Roadway, 6. Railway* and *7. Airways.*

The rich industrial nations have contrived for themselves a *club of seven – G7.* It is important to note that '*G*' is the seventh letter in the English alphabet.

'The *G7 types*' have made people at large believe that everyone's life depends on business, accounts, prices and profits to such an extent, that we tend to side line all other aspects. That the rich (*and successful*) have associated with the number seven, gives the number a halo in today's commercial world. That is why all attention seekers find favor with the number seven in the titles of their work or names of products.

Professionals, from publishing companies to lawyers, hotels and restaurants, casinos to cafes; everybody is climbing on the bandwagon of seven. Any Tom, Dick or Harry uses the number seven to add muscle to their presentation and gets away with it. The authors that have used the number seven in the title of their books are not a few hundred, but many thousands. Just to name a few:

- ABC of One to Seven
- The Secret Seven
- Home by Seven_
- The Seven Lives of Men
- The Science of Seven Cultures
- Seven Theories of Human Society
- The Seven Spiritual Laws of Success
- The Seven Sins of Memory

The Book Title list is endless and visibly growing...

The abuse of the Number Seven is so rampant, that it is *scary*. And, without any check for its usage, its abuse is growing alarmingly. In a bookstore it is nauseatingly obvious. As already touched upon, look at the non-fiction section at any bookstore and every third book title has a *seven* in it.

Users of the number seven are cunning & calculative crusaders. The problem is that they are endorsing the wrong. They use the number seven only when it is difficult for the average person to check the validity of their statement. And this is not exactly a new thing. It has been prevalent since the middle of 20th century.

Only to bring a number seven in the title; legendary Irving Wallace delinked the subject and title for a book, and titled his novel 'seven minutes'. The main subject of the novel has nothing to do with numeral seven. The use of the number seven by Mr Wallace was arbitrary, just his choice.

A literary critique in a protest against the title 'Seven Minutes' wrote, *"I always just assumed that '7 Seconds of Love' was the average duration of the male orgasm. Please enlighten me before I drown in a sea of sexual guilt!"* Interestingly, even in this critique, he employs the numeral seven, although sarcastically.

I would like you to compare this use of the number seven to recent use by some drug companies and populist websites. They have announced that latency time in sexual contact for a normal man is seven minutes. Since this is seemingly plausible and almost all people are incapable of verifying this; to them, the number seven is doing the trick of convincing that the statement is a *fact.* And in the process, rendering millions of men an inferiority complex; and luring them needlessly towards drugs and therapies.

The investment in the number seven as a marketing tool or in inducting it as a brand ambassador, must be worth a lot; particularly for the Europeans and the Americans. They apparently noticed the possibility that the succeeding generations might not take the number seven in the same light, and that their investment might go down the waste pipe. Hence, they planned on developing the liking for the number seven in children right from the start.

They compelled *Snow White* to have *seven dwarfs* and *Sinbad* to take up only *seven voyages*. They saw to it that the ducks that went in muddy water were seven in number; The serpent adorned seven heads; only seven kids meet the wolf; A father cursed to convert his seven children into seven crows and Madonna (*the writer*) in her book '*Yakov and Seven Thieves*', found it only right to force seven slippery scoundrels. The princesses in the fairy tales remained under a spell *for seven years*, and the boots of the famous cat--the *Marquis de Carabas*--were seven-leagued.

All accept that Children are unbiased; and their responses are pure. Thus, if children like seven; God must like seven or that it is just natural to like seven. For decades, the marketing men have connected the number seven with 'good' things and thereby succeeded in brainwashing children into liking number seven. It was natural that these children carried the liking of number seven into adulthood. Thus, the marketing men have, in addition to present children, have the present adults (previously children) under the spell of number seven. Now both, the children and the adults seem to accept that the number seven is likable or rather lovable. And that too without any reason, cause, history, association, and any other thing.

Wait, my above hypothesis may be incorrect and that it is possible that children like the number seven for some other obscure reason. I also cannot rule out that the number seven, by itself, is lovable.

Whichever alternative you accept; that association with number seven strengthens anything you place it with, is nothing short of truth!

Your limitation; it is only your imagination.
~ Guru Number Seven

7

⌑ Interlude
WHY INCLUDE TRUTHS?

Almost all books of collection of interesting realities have titles like, 'The Book of Facts', 'The Random Facts', The Awesome Facts, and 'The Thousand Facts'. Their titles make it obvious that the books are all about fascinating facts. Hardly anyone claims to introduce interesting truths. But often, they do present some 'truths' alongside the 'real' facts. Apparently, they do not consider the difference between a 'fact' and a 'truth'; as something worth taking in to account. For them, this is a non-issue. They seem to believe that, most people do not distinguish between the truths and the facts, and don't care.

I think the difference between truths and facts is important. A fact called a truth; or a truth called a fact; both send wrong messages.

Some truths, like facts, are also interesting, fascinating and informative in their own way. Exceptions apart, most truths have a positive energy. The truths are a part of everyday life just like the facts. This is why, I have chosen to place many 'truths' along with the facts. When we know which realities are 'facts' and which are 'truths'; then their information not only adds to your GK, making you knowledgeable; it can also make you fully aware of the reality; it can enlighten you, so to speak.

It is not very difficult to understand the difference between a fact and a truth. Let us understand the difference, before it becomes a nagging worry.

- A fact is a perception of reality. A truth is a perception which matches reality.

- Fact is basically something that exists/existed, or is/was present in reality. These are the things that can actually be verified, as well as proven by the other senses. Truth is what a person has come to believe. If he believes that something is true, then it is true. A 'truth' is something which depends on a person's perspective and experience.

- Facts are concrete realities that no amount of reasoning will change. Facts are not created; facts are simply acknowledged. Truths, as opposed to fact, are much more fluid and more malleable. Truths are those things that are not simply acknowledged, but must be discovered, or created.

- Truth: a fact or belief that is accepted as true. Fact: a thing that is proved to be true.

Why Include Truths?
"It is a Fact that Truths can be interesting".

Clarification

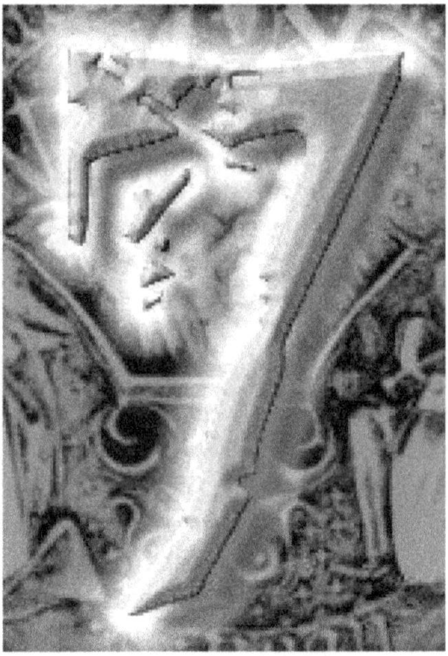

Is then, the number seven, a mystical number representing visions, dreams, and contemplation? Perhaps there is something deep and profound behind all these *sevens*, something just calling out for us to discover it. On the other hand, it might be nothing but a *Pythagorean coincidence*. Nevertheless, the '*Number Seven*' definitely demands a closer inspection to clear the ambiguity surrounding it.

In this setting, we must not overlook an interesting fact that when they took up to study the 'ambiguity'; two scholars, Mr W. Empson and Mr Elliot Perlman, both independently came out with a Book titled '*Seven types of ambiguities*'.

For starters, I know that Arithmetic does not love the number seven. Mathematically the number seven must find least occurrences compared to all other basic numerals (*0,1,2,3,4,5,6,8 and 9*). It is less used in all such matters as business, accounts, prices, or even at ordering required copies. It is neither very small, akin to the number three, nor a multiple of anything. It is also not a half or a quarter of any unit like a dozen. You hardly will find a product sold in a 'pack of seven'.

We know that a single hand finger count can easily show all numbers from one to five; like a '*two*' or a '*four*'. A seven cannot be displayed by a single hand finger count. We seldom realize that the number seven requires the use of both hands for communication. Yet another reason, seven would be less used or seen.

Due to its place in the Decimal or Binary systems, it is understandable that the number '*Seven*' should naturally find minimal use in Arithmetic and all its applications. Inevitably, number seven is less used and much less seen in arithmetical applications. And what is less seen and used becomes 'less important', goes without saying.

The www information highway proves that the number seven is no special item. The results of the search for numbers through engines like *Google* show that the number seven is not in the top ten numbers most used in the entire web-world.

Whether it is *Google*, *Yahoo* or any other specialized search engine like *WebQuest*, the number of entrée's for number seven indicate that it is neither special, nor extra popular.

A question naturally pops up; Is there really nothing magical about the number '*seven'*?

In reality, despite all that I have earlier penned here, rainbow colors are not seven; they are an infinite number. We all know the famous experiment of *Sir Isaac Newton*, which shows that when light passes through a prism, it breaks down into its components and shows a band of colors. Anyone looking at the colors created by a prism or a rainbow will see literally thousands of colors that blend into each other. Nevertheless, we think that the rainbow has seven colors. It was Sir Isaac Newton, who picked out seven as the number of colors that formed the rainbow, only because he thought that this number had a mystical value. The number seven was; well and truly; a fancy of Sir Isaac.

Seven musical notes do not represent the only way to divide the musical octave. Western music has twelve notes in an Octave. Since we designate five of them as 'sharp' or 'flats'; it looks as if there are just seven. In Indian music, a band of twenty-two Shrutis' cover the spectrum of sound in an Octave. But 'Swaras' (The equivalent of Notes – used for teaching and producing music on instruments) are seven. It is very likely that everybody's choice of seven, is only so, because all are comfortable with number seven.

Earlier in the book I have connected number seven with many things such as, Layers of atmosphere, Layers of Earth, Entities involved in Human fertilization, Layers of skin, Parts of the Eye, and Ear and a few others. I have just selected to present all these in seven parts, types, or quantity. All could also be described in others ways which may not be of seven items. What I have written are facts, but then, there can be other ways to divide the atmosphere, the ear, the eye, the skin wherein the number of parts could be any number. Just like Sir Isaac Newton, it has been my discretion to use number seven. And like his, mine did well too.

Take the case of classification of musical instruments. Not everyone classifies them into *seven*. Actually, most use the following four:

- String Instruments
- Wind Instruments
- Brass Instruments
- Percussion Instruments

Consider the case of the already-discussed group of stars called *the Pleiades* or *Seven Sisters*. The very unusual thing is that only 6 stars are visible to the bare eye, however almost every culture tells stories of 7 stars! The Thai call it *Seven Chucks*. The North American Indians believe that the Pleiades consisted of seven stars. The aborigines, the 'Iroquois of New York' explain that out of seven (brothers) one fell back to Earth and hence we see six. The Wyandot Indians explain that out of the seven sisters; one married a mortal. She and her mortal husband must sit in the back and so are not easily visible.

That there are seven continents and seas is also debatable, because the division is baseless and arbitrary. The most obvious example is the dividing line between Asia and Europe.

Somehow all want to cling to number seven. I am sure, it won't take a genius to realize that all such naming is just a *personal thing*!

There is nothing spiritual about the number *seven* in the Bible. Its frequent use is a consequence of the logic that 'when spoken in familiar terms to the reader; the message reaches completely'. The important point is not seven, or eight, or any other number. If there were eight days in the week, then, in the Bible, the eighth would be the day of rest.

The Bible itself, in Chapter 14, describes how Daniel was to be thrown in a cell with seven lions for seven days; thereby refuting the claim that '*seven*' is holy or permanently associated with the good or lucky.

In Mayan Mythology the number seven is important; but surprisingly, the numeral is associated with the 'evil' or with 'what must be destroyed'. Mayan Mythology states that the world was lorded over by *the evil and arrogant 'Seven Macaw'*. It further states that for the development of good humans, the role of Seven Macaw had to be ended.

In the early Greek (Hippocratic) tradition of Medicine, the number seven rules the illnesses of the body, with painful illness lasting 7, 14 or 21 days.

In the popular fairy-tale '*The Son of Seven Mothers*' by Flora Annie Steel (*1847-1929*), the seven are certainly unlucky.

The Swiss are noted for being neutral. Nevertheless, in the case of the number seven; the Swiss legend of 'The Seven Dwarfs' is a tale whose message is clear – seven is not golden; it is rather 'very unlucky'. In the story, the seven good dwarfs get killed, after doing a good deed, solely because they number *seven.*

Then there's an old English rhyme about crows and magpies that links the number seven with *Satan.* The rhyme reads: *"One means anger, Two means mirth, Three, a wedding, Four, a birth, Five is heaven, Six is hell, and Seven is the very devil himself."*

The Babylonian poem of Seven is all of Evil spirits. (R.C. Thompson translates) *"The first is the South wind, ... The second is a dragon, ... The third is a grim leopard, ... The fourth is a terrible Shibbu, ... The fifth is a furious Wolf, ... The sixth is a rampant beast, ... The seventh is a storm, an evil wind, which takes vengeance,"*

The number seven also leans on the *'negative side'* in the following:

- The beast has seven horns
- The seven deadly sins.
- Seven witches make a coven.

"And what the hell"; similar to the sky and the heaven; *the hell* also has seven levels: (*Torment | Repentance | Dementia | Misery | Contemn | Tribulation | and Dissolution)*.

The '*Mahayana Lotus Sutra*' says that seven types of occurrences that cause the seven types of disasters are the result of slandering the 'True Law'.

The cruel judge of the Bob Dylan song also has seven curses: *"These be seven curses on a judge so cruel ... and that seven deaths shall never kill him"*

Mahatma Gandhi listed only seven 'Deadly Sins' and called them the 'Seven Blunders of the World'. They are:

1. Wealth without Work
2. Pleasure without Conscience
3. Science without Humanity
4. Knowledge without Character
5. Politics without Principle
6. Commerce without Morality and,
7. Worship without Sacrifice.

That the Earth fancies number seven; as a positive do-gooder; is 'my' fantasy. Following seven are also creations of the Earth: 1. Storms. 2. Tornadoes. 3. Earthquakes. 4. Volcanoes. 5. Floods – Avalanche – Landslide. 6. Droughts – Heat Waves. 7. Wild Fires.

Sanderson Beck, the American author, has listed - the *Seven Deadly 'isms'* - this list is easy to agree with – *1. Sexism, 2. Racism, 3. Imperialism, 4. Militarism, 5. Materialism, 6. Dogmatism,* and *7. Egoism.*

I have seen the good associations of the number seven when I was looking for them and found almost equal instances of bad associations as I slipped into a 'negative' mood.

All wonders being seven in number, is a wonder in itself. There is no logic for limiting and fixing up selected items to number seven. If you examine the lists of these seven wonders it can easily be seen that the lists do not have any logic for selection or exclusion of great achievements nor do they have for the list to be of seven.

The seventy-odd nominations listed by the Swiss organization for '*New Seven Wonders*', are predominantly old to very old. Every reader would find something missing even in this list; something that should have been there. I am sure the reader would question why a particular feat is listed. I want to ask – Why the list has to be of only seven things; not one more, not one less.

The more I look for these negative '*sevens*', the more I see them... *'I am confused'.* And my being just confused, is becoming the top understatement of this book. That takes us back to the main topic of this review, 'Is the number seven 'good' or 'bad'?'

Furthermore, unlike the case of 'ambiguities', I have not found any book on *seven types of 'confusions'* to explain my fusion with and confusion about Guru Number Seven.

Poets are overzealous and some can take extreme routes. Their works, like this one by David Bowie and Reeves Gabrels, which was written for a computer game – the Nomad Soul - somehow touch upon the 'jurisdiction' of Guru number Seven in its unique way.

"I forgot what my father said, ...
I got Seven days to live my life or
Seven ways to die, ..."

About these contrasting faces of the number seven; I am certainly not going to just sit and do nothing like these seven old men, ...

Even animals can think of something to do when they are *seven.*

An adult Human is made up of about
7,000,000,000,000,000,000,000,000,000
(7 octillion) atoms.

The Octillion is a very large number,
but is still far closer than infinity,
and more importantly,
it is measurable.

Reality

In Sanskrit 'सप्त' (Sapta) is the name for 'seven,' It is 'Hepta' in Greek. These languages led to number 7 being named 'Septem' in Latin, and arrived in English as 'Seven'.

Hey readers, a Seven, is just a numeral, a number used to count and account in Arithmetic. Such Numerals, 0, 1, 2, 3, 4, 5, 6, 7, 8 and 9; are the most common system for the symbolic representation of digits in the world today, and called Hindu–Arabic numerals.

Seven in Hebrew is 'Shivah', often mistaken for *'Saba',* which signifies - *being full, satisfying, and complete*). This could be the background why the western world considers the number seven; a number of fullness, perfection, and completeness.

Numeral systems have progressed from the use of tally marks, more than 40,000 years ago. The Babylonians had probably the first set of glyphs for numerals around BC 2000.

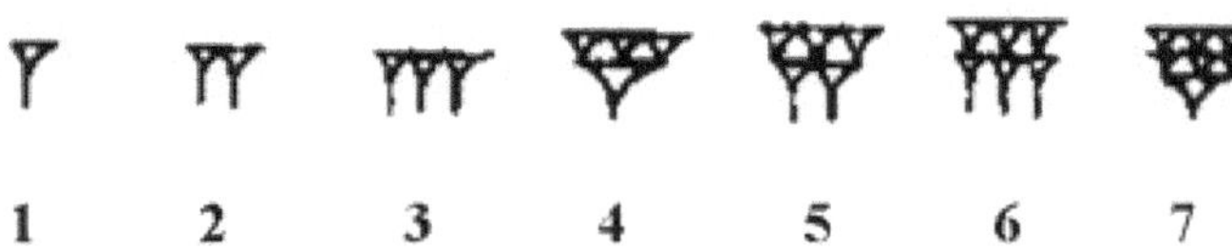

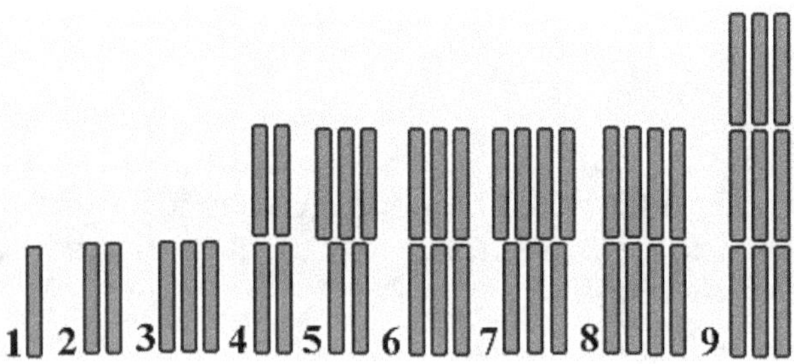

The Aegean and ancient Egyptian Numerals.

Mayan Numerals: A horizontal line meant five and a dot meant one.

The Brahmi (ancient Indian) numerals (3rd century BCE) are the direct graphic ancestors of the modern Indian and Hindu–Arabic numerals.

	1	2	3	4	5	6	7	8	9
10^0	𑁒	𑁓	𑁔	𑁕	𑁖	𑁗	𑁘	𑁙	𑁚

The 'modern' or 'western' numerals actually originated in India where they had multiple forms. From among them the Arabs chose, what appeared to them as most useful. The Arabs when speaking Arabic, called them the 'Indian numbers', proves the origin. The reason the digits are more commonly known as 'Arabic numerals' in Europe and the Americas, is because they were introduced to Europe in the 10th century by Arabic-speakers of North Africa.

The shape of western numeral seven evolved from a Hindu beginning, via Arabic to its present form. In the beginning, various Hindus wrote number 7 more or less in one stroke as a curve that looks like an uppercase '*J*' upside down. The contribution of the Western and the Arabic men was mainly to introduce straight lines.

The number seven has settled as a two-stroke character consisting of a horizontal upper line joined at its right with a line going down towards the bottom left corner, a line that is slightly curved in some font variants.

There is an interesting history to the numerals settling to their present form.

By the turn of the 11th century, a variety of forms were in use to express numerals or digits. Each based on independent validation with equal or no logic. A uniform set of numerals was the need of trans European trade. The shapes based on the count of angles emerged as the commonly accepted numeral set. Being related to Trigonometry helped; because Trigonometry, the branch of mathematics which emerged in 3rd century BC and in about ten centuries established itself as the best validator of the most complex mathematical issues like astronomical events and calculations. The impasse was solved and the western world had a uniformly shaped numeral. Look at these Numerals, particularly the seven.

1 2 3 4 5 6 7 8 9 0

The logic of angles: When reduced to straight lines all number shapes have angles equal to its digit.

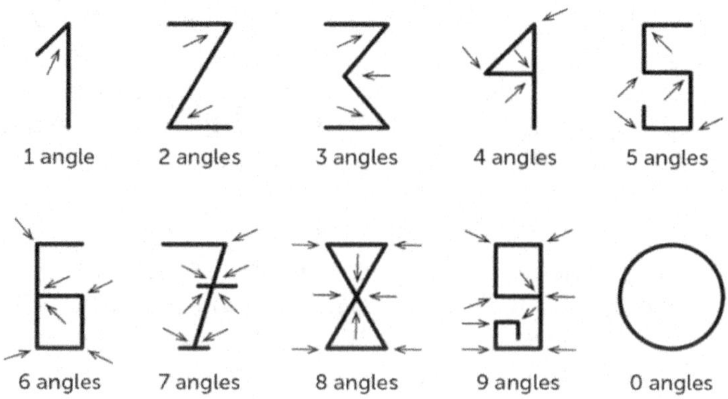

Only number seven is the odd one in this story; with a dash in the middle of the vertical.

If you check with the chart showing the appearance of numerals on the earlier page, you will notice that the form of number seven never had a horizontal line, a dash, in the middle or the base of its vertical.

The dash in the middle, a vestige now, was demanded by those who had suffered due to mistakes in reading numeral Seven (as numeral 1); as well as in case of numerals Two and Zero (letter Z and letter O respectively).

The ad hoc horizontal lines, the dashes crossing the vertical, seem to be added; by the promoters of a uniform set of numerals; so that the form of numeral seven has seven angles (corners) in it; and thereby ruling out objections if any; about its belonging to the set. Nowhere before or after; these lines, the dashes, are seen in common use; except by some financial accountants and military men, who used it in the pre-typewriter days to avoid mistakes due to bad handwriting.

With the Colonial rule over most of the civilised world, these numerals became the standard worldwide. After the end of the Colonial rule, most independent countries like India, continue to use and officially accept the use of the 'Hindu-Arabic' set of numerals for convenient communication; although they have a separate official national language and which has its own set of numerals.

"Games purely based on numbers tell a telling tale of 'Lucky Seven"

In the games of Housie, Bingo, Raffle, etc.; the winning numbers are generally announced in the presence of bettors. To make the announcements of numbers interesting; the announcers use the simile or the attributes of numbers. Any Housie, Bingo or Raffle player would find the following lines familiar –

"Starting point – Number One"
"Legs – Eleven"
"Bamboo Door – Fifty-Four"
"Grandma's age –Eighty-five"
"Luckeeeee – single number – seven."

“Lucky?” Is ‘seven’ lucky? It is obvious that ‘*Eleven*’ looks like a pair of legs; ‘*Fifty-four*’ gets its nickname ‘*Bamboo door*’ from the famous song... etc. But, why is ‘*Seven*’ lucky?

In casinos, the slot machine is famously known for its lucky 7, where a person can win a big prize by getting three sevens together.

The cover of a Perry Mason mystery novel shows both dice combinations leading to the number Seven, 5+2 on top, and 4 + 3 on the side faces of the dice. The legs are also portrayed like the number seven.

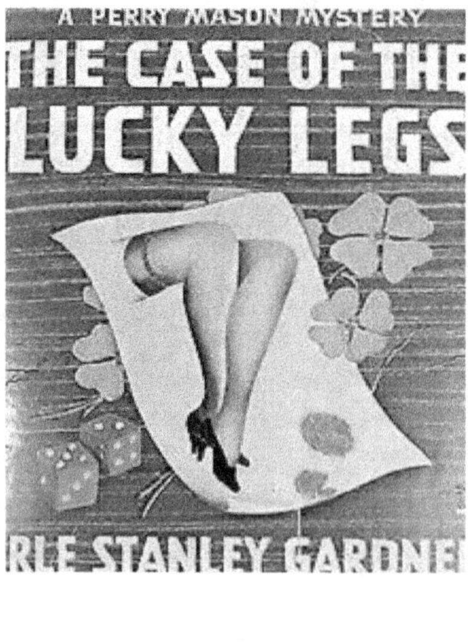

Even the Hoodoo (witchcraft) has joined the 7 brigades. Naming a soap *'Lucky 7'*, and repeating number 7 many times on the packaging of 'Lucky seven soap', have promoted the *'luckiness'* of the number like many others, that the average person has accepted it without further query.

Hoodoo packaging of 'Lucky 7 Soap'.

The Japanese 'Seven Gods of Luck'

The Japanese *'Seven Gods of Luck'*, a group of seven popular deities are one of the many myths to add strength to the belief in luckiness of seven. All deities are of good fortune and happiness.

'The association of number seven with luckiness is so commonplace, that it is no wonder, the announcer of the numbers in the game of Housie or Raffle, ***called the number seven, 'lucky'****.*

The fad of number 7 has reached so high that if you use the number seven; you can find a use for useless scrap items and make money from it. The large sale of the 'seven lucky artifacts'; in reality an assortment of *seven* useless scrap items, proves the point. One such 'lucky' set of seven absolutely useless scrap items is: wishbone, used horseshoe, four-leaf clover, rabbit's foot, Shark's Tooth, Bodhi Seeds and Tiger's Claw.

What has the number seven got to do with *luck*? This question at hand is not fully answered yet. That the number Seven is Lucky may be a myth. Myths, like truths, are not required to have validation nor can they produce any. Yet, we may require validation, since we still have not confirmed whether it is a myth.

Dice games or the dice may have the answer; because winning at Dice games is more dependent on luck than in any other game.

In the dice games, the *'lucky seven'* and the reality is a paradoxical pair. A gambler is surely lucky' when he wins even though he has placed his bet on a least probable result. But if his bet is placed on a number that has the highest likelihood of winning (called *'a favourite'* in gambling terms) and he wins, we cannot say he or the number is 'Lucky'.

The fact that gamblers have named the 'seven' to be 'lucky'; implies that they believe it is a less probable number in a dice game. The reality however, is the opposite; the number seven has the highest probability.

Take a look at the probabilities... We know that the total of the numbers on the top sides of both dice is the achieved number.

Out of the total 36 possibilities, the total of two dice tops will be 7 in six possibilities; a higher chance than any other number.

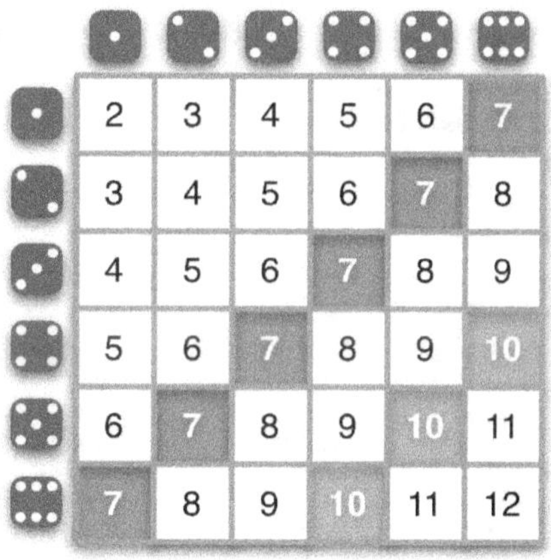

Numbers 6 and 8 have the next best prospect of five; followed by 5 & 9 who have four chances; and finally, numbers 2 and 12 have only one chance each. Therefore, in dice games if one bets on and gets a 2 or a 12, for him, 2 or 12 would be *'lucky'*.

In the games played with two six-sided dice; with highest chance; the number 7 should be a *'favourite'* and not the *'lucky'* number. And getting this 'favourite' number one has a prospect of only 6 out of 36, or 1 in 6, or about 17%. The remaining 83% possibility is with the Casino.

Smart casino men know this well and lure people with all kinds of attractions.

Remarkably, the gambling fraternity is not isolated in embracing the number seven. The school of Guru number Seven has an astonishing Alumni.

Let's go and meet the Alumni.

....

"I don't gamble, nor do I recommend gambling in any form because gambling gets you nowhere. I hope you stay away."

Justification

"Winning isn't everything,
but wanting to win is."
~Vince Lombardi

On second thought, I do not think the number seven is less used compared to other numbers. I see so many things in our day-to-day life; related to the number seven that puts a serious question mark on the *validity* of the statistics of search engines. I also do not think that the number seven has negative vibes. On the contrary, I now feel confident that the Number Seven is the most-liked by all and even the most used number of all. Whether someone uses the number Seven as a Cardinal number, Ordinal number or Denominate (*measure*) number, *IT ALWAYS SEEMS TO EVOKE ATTENTION*!!!

For me; musing with the amazing and amusing seven is now unavoidable. A question comes forth. Does the number seven have any quality for success?

Perhaps the number seven getting the tag 'a success getter' lies in the saying, 'Nothing succeeds like success'. In support, stands the pair of the unchanged secret flavouring 7X, and the success of Coca-Cola since the turn of 19th century.

Movie moguls like the number; *and why not*? Almost all movies with the number seven are successful. The movies *'Seven-year itch', 'Seven brides for seven brothers', 'The magnificent seven', 'Seven Girlfriends', 'The Seventh sign'* of *Demi Moore...*, to name a few.

Code of John Dee

Code name of James Bond

'OO7', the code name of the super-spy James Bond, has an interesting origin.

It was the code used by *'John Dee'* an advisor/spy to the British Queen Elizabeth-I. The two 00's signifying – for your eyes only; and a '7' giving protection by extending over.

Famed Japanese director *Akira Kurosawa* also used the number seven in the title of his movie '*Seven Samurai*'. After its success, he said, *"Seven has a 'secret bond' with success."*

I would like to explain the phenomenon of the number seven by the slot theory in modern psychiatry. It visualizes that total human STM (*Short term memory*) is divided in seven slots; each of which can contain a packet of a particular information. After the seven are full, any additional information demanding to be stored, has to get rid of one of the existing packets; because the slots are only seven.

Key situations in business negotiations demand appreciation and an analytical understanding of the offer from the opposite side. To succeed it is necessary to arm oneself with maximum knowledge and to understand fully the offer details. '*What happened a minute ago*' becomes extremely important. In other words, Short Term Memory (STM) becomes all important.

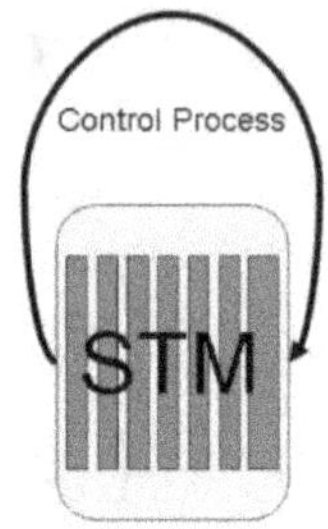

The number seven plays a role in the Short-Term Memory since it represents the span of 'immediate memory'. Most people remember seven items from a single presentation. Only a few can remember more than seven items of a single sequence. One of the interesting aspects of this memory is that the amount of information per item has little effect on the span of memory.

George Miller, the cognitive psychologist, in his article, 'The Magical Number Seven; Plus-or-Minus Two: Some Limits on Our Capacity for Processing Information', showed that the amount of information that people can process and remember, is often limited to about seven items. Miller called this, the digit span.

In his article 'Mind - A Sticky Seven-Dimensional Phase Space', Dr Chris McKinstry, a theoretical psychologist says "I believe the mind to be a fractal pattern on the surface of a seven-dimensional hypersphere."

According to *Carla Rieger*'s statistics, the average adult attention span is actually only *seven seconds*. That's right! Every seven seconds, you go away somewhere; you think about something else.

Allyson Lewis, the author of the book 'The Seven Minute Difference', through her workshops for three years found a similar finding: That the average corporate executive, has an attention-span of just seven minutes.

Most psychologists accept the following - the seven-point rating scale, the seven categories for absolute judgment, the seven objects in the span of attention, and the seven digits in the span of immediate memory. They inform: *"Ask a number of people to give you any number between one and ten, and most will choose seven. Ask people to name their favourite number between one and ten, and again, most will say seven."*

Ask someone to repeat back to you exactly what you say. Begin with four digits chosen at random, e.g., *6, 6, 2, 5*. Then give them five digits, e.g., *5, 8, 4, 5, 0*, then six, and so on. Carry on increasing the number of digits until they make a mistake. The longest number of digits most people get completely right; their digit span; is *seven digits*.

Perhaps the memory span is the reason behind the acceptability of the earlier seven-digit telephone numbers and how people find it difficult to remember the new *9 or10* digit numbers. The old car number plates had seven figures and they were comfortable to remember with or without alphabets. Now with higher digits almost no one remembers the full car numbers.

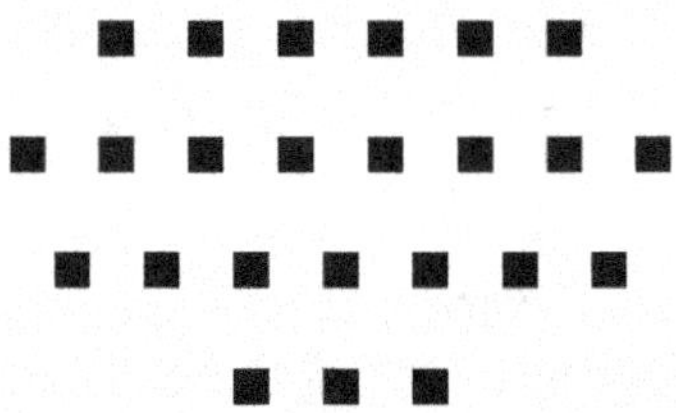

Show some people a pattern of dots for a very short time - *just one fifth of a second, for instance* - and ask them to count the number of dots. If the number of dots is less than seven, they will be right almost every time, but with more than seven, they will make lots of mistakes.

Thus, the number seven borders on the line of the possible and the impossible. Its place keeps you guessing. If the number seven does not make it, it is surprising; and if it gets it, it's still a surprise. And *surprise* is one of the key ingredients of *joy*. If seven brings happiness, then so be it. Why then, I am questioning this worldwide love for the number seven?

I am beginning to get relieved. There is nothing wrong with me because I like the number seven. Strangely, if I did not like the number seven, it would not mean that something is wrong with me. Either way, I must be a normal person; and now, I am finally convinced that I am.

The 7-digit span of short-term memory, explains why many things are seven; from colours in rainbow to musical notes. I feel like the '*Hootchie Cootchie Man*' and want to sing the *Song of Seven* confirming the seven notes.

"On the seventh hour, of the seventh day, of the seventh month, the seven doctors say - he was born for good luck, that you'll see. I got seven hundred dollars. Don't you mess with me cause I'm the Hootchie Cootchie man..." ≈ Willie Dixon.

I also feel like Mark Chagall and dream that I have seven supple fingers of a creative person who can count seven with a single hand finger count.

(Part of Self Portrait by Mark Chagall)

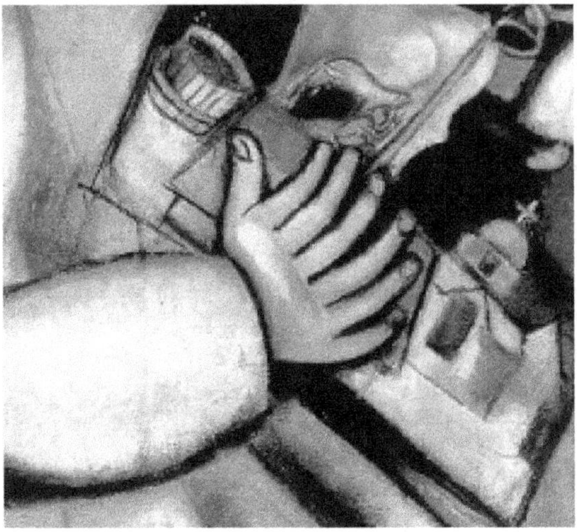

From the desk of
SEVEN

Dear Author,

You have penned detailing all the fascinating facts and truths that showed up as you stayed with me. The truth is that the collection includes all the keys required to unlock any impasse that one may have. That is enough.

You don't have to be better than everybody else all the time; The 'passing criteria' for this 'exercise of life' is that you have to be better than you thought you could be.

You did it; and I think it will make you happy

"The sign of intelligence is that you are constantly wondering.

Idiots are always dead sure about every damn thing they are doing in their life."

~ *Sadhguru*

Lessons Learned

A path from ‘nobody’ to ‘somebody’.

I am happy. Whether you believe that I received a letter from Guru number Seven does not matter. My happiness itself, indicates that I have successfully completed the undertaken task and that I have achieved.

However small, this type of achievement brings in changes in you. And what you become by achieving your targets or aims is far more important.

By taking Number seven as a Guru, I have reached the goal of writing a book of fascinating facts & truths. I have shared with you most of the facts found. If I could accomplish so much by taking an abstract primary arithmetical number as my Guru, think what all will happen if you take any Guru of your liking.

The change in me begins with, 'I forgot that I had missed the bus', that's for sure.

When presented with an assembly of facts and truths; now I seem to:

- Understand what they are;
- Comprehend their uniqueness;
- Rationalize their message;
- Put them in their rightful place.
- And I am able to enjoy them at the same time.

And what did I do to get this bonanza?

In this quest,
I tried hitting at all corners,
Every time I took an aim and fired a salvo,
whether it found a pot of gold,
was not my worry. Because...

*"If you don't aim at something,
you'll never hit anything."*

Furthermore, an old Marathi proverb egged me on... *'Prayatne walooche kana ragadata telahi gale."*

It means that if you try hard enough, keep on trying, you may make an impossible, a possible; and squeeze out oil from sand.

The wise words of a centenarian philanthropist, *W. Clement Stone,* have come true: *"Aim for the moon. If you miss, you may hit a star".*

With Guru number Seven,
I didn't miss much,
and reached my goal.

"And, So Can You."

For this, at times, I had to think 'Out of the Box'. Many guides support the idea of thinking out of the box so strongly as if, this is the only way to go and if you think out of the box, the solution is yours for the asking. I don't think it is the only way to go. 'Follow in footsteps' or 'Follow the well-trodden path' are the proven rules; while 'Thinking out of the Box' is a lovable exception, rather a never to be ignored alternative.

I was not in a hurry to lock up facts and truths or to place them on an unreachable high pedestal; I always left a door open for reconsideration, correction, and change.

I had a revelation: 'Imagine that you are jailed, chained, hands and feet tied to a cross and made fully immobile; even then, you are not powerless. There are certain powers that your captor can never take away from you. Rather, except death, probably no one can'.

William Shakespeare explains this in his unique way – he pens - *"The robbed that smiles, steals something from the thief."*

Contrary to the popular belief that we have five senses, we all have twenty senses: sound, sight, touch, smell and taste. The other fifteen are: balance, acceleration, temperature, pain, proprioception *(awareness of the place and movement of the body),* sexual stimulation, time, suffocation, thirst, hunger, respiratory rate, vomiting, itching, blushing and fullness. I had to to put in action all senses at disposal, and then, observe, reason and place the finding in the context. This is how I gained comprehensive awareness; a must if you want to be wholesomely sensible about anything.

I realized that eventually, all these recognitions and actions turn into powers that makes us all, potentially limitless. Walt Whitman confirms this fact in his inimitable way, in his 'Song of Myself' (*Leaves of Grass*)

"Of the earth, You, whoever you are!...
......
Each of us limitless-
each of us with
his or her right on earth,
......
Divine I am inside and out and I
Make holy whatever I touch or
Am touched from..."
......

I have realized that I have learned only a bit out of the universe. But I did learn and have become a little more 'well-read', than I was earlier. I have progressed. More importantly, I have broken the shackles of an impasse. That was the goal anyway.

In all this journey, willingness to learn new things, and accepting the newly learned, emerge as the pair of tracks on which your progress rests. The result obviously depends on *'how'* we learn.

As stated earlier; before taking number seven as my Guru; 'what and how to learn from the infinite ocean of total consciousness', was the stumbling block'. Now, I have learned, *'how to learn'.*

I understand that, a lot of what we learn depends on what we choose to unlearn and what we limit.

I have understood Albert Einstein when he cautions - "The only thing that interferes with my learning is my education *(which is restrictive, rather than permissive as it shoulod be).*"

Learn to unlearn. Scrutinise the many facts stuffed down your throat in the name of education, tradition etc. It is possible that some of them may be interfering with your learning.

To *'unlearn'* is important to all learning. Not only does it create the required space, but it removes blockages as well. The first to unlearn is this notion - *'I am different'*. No sir/madam, we are not different. We all know only a little. We all need to accept the need and be willing to learn new things.

To unlearn includes delinking. Sometimes a fact or a truth becomes good or bad only due to its link established with something/s by tradition or your past. These links are dangerous like a virus. When in doubt, sanitise all data. You will be happily surprised to find a very strong built-in antivirus within you.

What we should not forget, is that, not only the marketing men, but many other groups - social, religious, political and tradition-based, at some point in our life; create blocks or hurdles in the freethinking; by convincing us about something being a fact when it is not so.

Once you notice something amiss, '*sleep on it*' if you must, but don't forget to act. Once you remove the blocks – the things you have taken for granted as facts; you will be a lot more aware, and be able to put things in the right perspective.

Then let the world seem,

"Single dimensional as that of an infant,
Two dimensional as that of a kid;
Three dimensional as that of a young person,
Four dimensional as that of a connoisseur;
Five dimensional as that of an architect,
With a sixth sense as that of a poet or
A Seven dimensional of visionary physicists;

Our world, it actually remains unchanged,
In whichever scale we measure it with."

At work; understanding the dimensions; me.

Compendium

A Guru is the remover of darkness: In Sanskrit, 'Gu' means darkness, and 'Ru' means remover. Here, what conceals the light of awareness is 'Darkness'. The enlightenment principle that aids one in the path to realization is the Guru.

For your Guru to be effective, you should know who he is, and completely submit to him, This is best explained by a two line Vedic verse.

गुरूर्ब्रम्हा गुरूविष्णुः गुरूर्देवो महेश्वरः

गुरूः साक्षात् परब्रम्ह तस्मै श्रीगुरवे नमः

"Gurur-Brahma, Guru Vishnu, Gurur-Devo Maheshwara; Guru sakshat, param Brahma, tasmai shri guravay namah || "

The force of creation – Brahma; the force of preservation – Vishnu; and the force of transformation or destruction – Maheshwara; all are our Gurus.

The guru present and already connected to you is the 'Guru Sakshat' and a guru that is beyond the beyond is 'Param Brahma'.

(However),

I make my offering to the beautiful; remover of my darkness and my ignorance; ***my Guru***; it is to 'you' that I bow.

I will never know whether you will choose to seek more for yourself, or just enjoy this reading of fascinating facts. Both options are fine by me. But if you choose to be an achiever, it would be nice for you to know the lessons learnt by me after accepting *'Guru number Seven'* as my Guru, with a different point of view and how you have similar opportunities.

I would like to take example of the sports; particularly the *ball games*. Imagine trying to play a ball game without the fixed size of the court or field; without any restrictions on the ball size and type; without any restriction of time; without any restriction on the size of the bat (*racket or stick*) and without restriction on who and how many to play with. It's just not possible to play a game, isn't it?

However, when you add all necessary restrictions, a game is on. One cannot play a good tennis game on the football field. Therefore, you must choose the game that you want to play and accept its rules and restrictions.

You should name 'what you want to do', a 'game', a 'goal', or 'love'. That way it is easier to identify with it. The unique set of restrictions, encompassing what you want to do, are the keys to the gateway of achievement. It deserves a name too. You may call the unique set of restrictions by any name; but I would strongly recommend calling it your Guru; 'The XYZ Guru'. I have called mine 'Number Seven'.

One should not forget that you need someone or a group to play with. You have to accept that they also want to play to win; that they have accepted the rules of the game and spirit of sportsmanship; therefore, you must respect their acceptance and reciprocate. It is then, you are certain to win their respect.

And then, it is not really important which game you choose; if your choice helps you, it's good enough.

Remember, when you learned to drive or ride a bicycle. In the beginning, it looked similarly complicated with many fronts to face. Soon you mastered them and now riding the bicycle or driving is as simple as walking. The interesting fact is that for a baby, learning to walk is far more complicated than learning to drive for grownups.

Face the facts by bringing out the child in you, giving up every preconceived notion, following humbly the senses, wherever and to whatever they lead you; only then; you will comprehend.

Truths are rarely pure and never simple. If it is someone else's truth, you are not obliged to accept it as a fact. A truth is not obliged to possibilities. A truth is not necessarily a true story; however, it can be an extremely useful good-doer.

A fact can change. It can change in time, by growth or decay, by development or destruction and birth or death.

The example of this, which I like best is:

Old Fact: You are a non-achiever.

Future Fact: You are an achiever.

Look at boundaries as agents that set you free. That's the play of the game.

"Play it well and you will achieve."

I am happy now, not only because now I have succeeded; but because my demonstration is fruitful.

I am happy because, now, when asked to choose; you would choose, "Yes, I can".

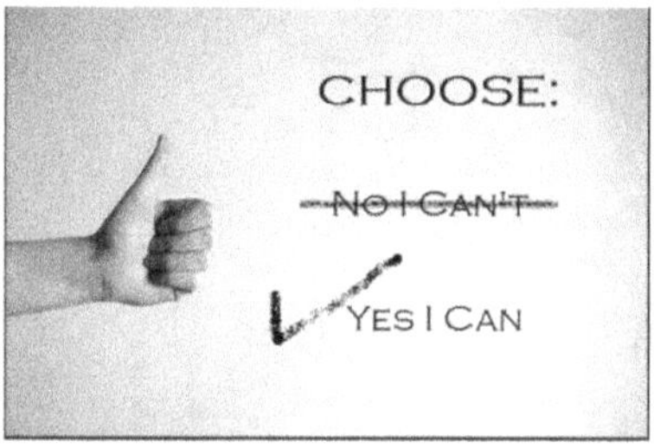

We have realized that

'I Can';
'You can';
'Everybody can';
is a truth, for one and all.

And when you succeed,
your truth will be a 'Fact' for you.

AMEN,

English, French, German, Italian, Croatian etc.

אָמֵן,

Hebrew

آمين,

Arabic

アーメン,

Japanese

สาธุ,

Thai

阿门,

Chinese simplified

तथास्तु.

Sanskrit, Marathi, Hindi

Epilogue

I am now in love Number seven, not only as my guru, but also as an entity. I also now know why Number seven loves me; the reason he accepted me as a student. The answer is, my assertions. Firstly, 'The one who demonstrates conveys more effectively' and Secondly, 'The boundaries (framework) set you free'. Both are very dear to him and number seven, Illustrates and manifests both these by his persona.

Number seven, settled as a two-stroke character, having a horizontal upper line; joined at its right end with another line going down angularly to the bottom of an imaginary rectangle (*presumed to have ratio of 1: 1.5 to 1.6 in 'portrait orientation*); and meeting the bottom line in the left half of bottom line.

Thus, the basic boundaries (terms of acceptance) are:

- Made up of primarily two lines.
- One horizontal at the top.
- The second a slanted vertical,
- The lines join at the right end of the upper line.
- The lines together create an angle

7

One would say, configuration of numeral seven is well defined; where is the freedom? As an alumnus of the school of Guru Number Seven, I would rather than getting closed out by the stated boundaries; become aware that there is/are no restriction on:

the lines being absolutely straight
the thickness of lines,
uniformity of thickness
fading out,
patterned lines
dotted lines
angle at meeting of lines
proportion, vertical vs. horizontal
adding lines
adding patterns
colours
textures
adding items to suite occasion
adding items to be attractive to a specific group
e.g., children
to add character of a font
strengthening open ends
... ...
... ...

You will find that the more you seek them, more freedom points will be visible to you.

And then, we always have the right to take some liberties with most of the things; as long as the liberties taken do not change the basics of the entity; or makes the perception of the entity seriously ambiguous.

The fonts used by computer software's; show the freedom available in spite of technical and commercial restrictions.

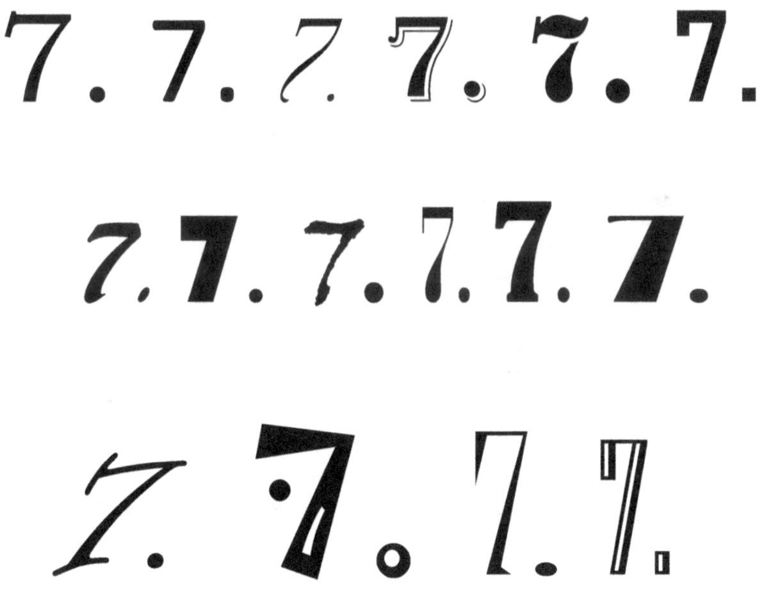

The commercial artists with their designs, leave no doubt about the freedom. Aren't these sevens beautiful?

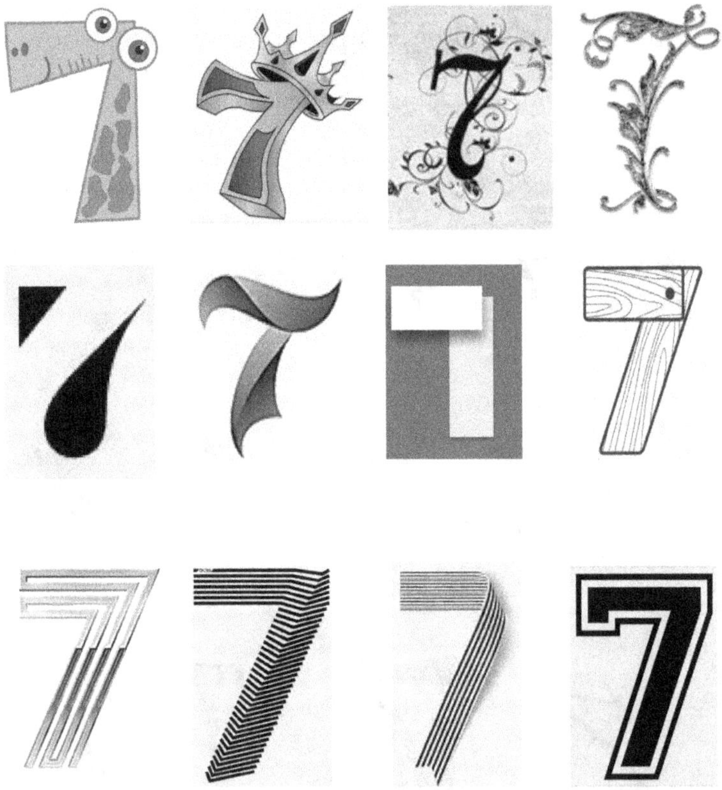

To end; all I can add is:

“Nothing is impossible;

the word actually spells, ‘I-m-possible’!”

About the Author:

VINAY CHANDE

B.Arch. (MSU-Ind), M. A. Arch. (UF-USA), F.I.I.A., F.I.V.

Unique and multiple viewpoints to observe and present things without prejudice, and living in the present; are hallmark of his style. His writings are fresh, fascinating, and yet simple; making reader wonder "why did I not think of this before?" In addition to practicing as an architect; he was a professor of Architecture and has travelled widely. He was born in 1947. He lives in Mumbai with wife. His two married daughters live in USA.

Email: gharandaz@gmail.com

Other Books by the author:

- The Book of Good Facts.

Facts for smart people to be smarter.

- The Smile, The Game Changer.

A biographical study of the 16th century born expression, and the hoax of smile of Mona Liza

- 'Disata Tase Aaste'.

A book of short stories in Marathi.

www.ingramcontent.com/pod-product-compliance
Lightning Source LLC
Chambersburg PA
CBHW062108160726
48282CB00026B/710
9789354450679